A Thrilling Narrative

The Civil War in the West

Series Editor: Daniel E. Sutherland

A Thrilling Narrative

The Memoir of a Southern Unionist

By Captain Dennis E. Haynes

Edited by Arthur W. Bergeron Jr.

The University of Arkansas Press

Fayetteville

2006

ISBN-10 1-55728-811-7
ISBN-13 978-1-55728-811-0

Manufactured in the United States of America

10 09 08 07 06 5 4 3 2 1

Designed by Liz Lester

♾ The paper used in this publication meets the minimum requirements of the American National Standard for Permanence of Paper for Printed Library Materials Z39.48-1984.

LIBRARY OF CONGRESS
CATALOGING-IN-PUBLICATION DATA

Haynes, D. E. (Dennis E.)
A thrilling narrative : the memoir of a Southern unionist / by Dennis E. Haynes ; edited by Arthur W. Bergeron Jr.
p. cm.
Includes bibliographical references and index.
ISBN 1-55728-811-9 (hardcover : alk. paper)
1. Haynes, D. E. (Dennis E.) 2. Louisiana—History—Civil War, 1861–1865—Personal narratives. 3. United States—History—Civil War, 1861–1865—Personal narratives. 4. Unionists (United States Civil War)—Louisiana—Biography. 5. Louisiana—History—Civil War, 1861–1865—Campaigns. 6. United States—History—Civil War, 1861–1865—Campaigns. 7. Red River Expedition, 1864. I. Bergeron, Arthur W. II. Title.
E510.H42 2006
973.7'170922763—dc22

2005028587

CONTENTS

Series Editor's Preface vii
Preface xi
Editor's Introduction xv

Introduction 3
Chapter 1 5
Chapter 2 13
Chapter 3 23
Chapter 4 37
Chapter 5 45
Chapter 6 53
Chapter 7 61
Chapter 8 67
Chapter 9 75
Chapter 10 81

APPENDICES

"Correspondence" 87
"The Reconstruction of States" 107
"Emigration to the Southern States" 115
"Extracts from the Journal of C. S. G. Clifton" 123

Notes 129
Bibliography 159
Index 165

SERIES EDITOR'S PREFACE

The Civil War in the West series has a single goal: To promote historical writing about the war in the western states and territories. It focuses most particularly on the Trans-Mississippi theater, which consisted of Missouri, Arkansas, Texas, most of Louisiana (west of the Mississippi River), Indian Territory (modern-day Oklahoma), and Arizona Territory (two-fifths of modern-day Arizona and New Mexico), but it also encompasses adjacent states, such as Kansas, Tennessee, and Mississippi, that directly influenced the Trans-Mississippi war. It is a wide swath, to be sure, but one too often ignored by historians and, consequently, too little understood and appreciated.

Topically, the series embraces all aspects of the wartime story. Military history in its many guises, from the strategies of generals to the daily lives of common soldiers, forms an important part of that story, but so, too, do the numerous and complex political, economic, social, and diplomatic dimensions of the war. The series also provides a variety of perspectives on these topics. Most important, it offers the best in modern scholarship, with thoughtful, challenging monographs. Secondly, it presents new editions of important books that have gone out of print. And thirdly, it premieres expertly edited correspondence, diaries, reminiscences, and other writings by witnesses to the war.

It is a formidable challenge, but by focusing on some of the least familiar dimensions of the conflict, the Civil War in the West series significantly broadens understanding of the nation's most dramatic story.

The role of the Southern home front in determining the outcome of the Civil War has attracted increasing—and deserved—attention over the past two decades. Historians have paid closer attention to the activities of noncombatants (both free and slave), the guerrilla war, and the interplay between politics, the economy, and society. Their discoveries have enriched our understanding of how and why the war was waged. Some of the most prominent and fruitful of this scholarship has dealt with Southern unionists, whose numbers and complex roles in the war have been shown to be more significant than previously thought. Long assumed to have been motivated largely by their opposition to slavery, and to have been of consequence only in the border states, we now know that unionists were far from monolithic in their political views, and that they populated the Deep South from Georgia to Texas.

The narrative of Dennis E. Haynes adds immeasurably to our knowledge of wartime Southern unionism. To begin with, its republication makes available a personal perspective that has been all but lost to students of the war. First published in 1866, only two copies are now known to exist. Haynes's account is also important because first-hand accounts of unionism in the Deep South are rare, especially so for the lower reaches of the Trans-Mississippi. Previous volumes in this series—most notably the wartime accounts of William Baxter, Albert W. Bishop, and William Monks—have provided unique perspectives on unionism in Arkansas and Missouri. Haynes confirms that strong unionist sentiment existed in Louisiana, too. He also shows, like Bishop and Monk, that not all unionists were passive victims of rebel oppression. It is true that thousands of unionist noncombatants suffered both legal and extralegal abuse at the hands of Confederate neighbors. They lost homes and property and often became refugees. However, nearly equal numbers fought back, either as guerrillas or as recruits in the Union army. Haynes chose the road of resistance, and the purposes, perspectives, and actions of men like him are crucial for a balanced view of the war's many military, political, and social dimensions. Further enhancing the innate value of Haynes's story is the superb editorial work of Dr. Arthur W. Bergeron Jr. An authority on the war in Louisiana, Bergeron has scrutinized every aspect of

Haynes's account. He points out where Haynes exaggerated or was in error, identifies people, places, and events in the story not fully explained by Haynes, and provides the historical context necessary for understanding both Haynes and the unionist community he represented. Thus Bergeron has not only recovered an important historical source, but he has also shown why Dennis Haynes must be regarded as a valuable interpreter of the unionist experience.

Daniel E. Sutherland
Series Editor

PREFACE

The *Narrative* of Dennis E. Haynes is one of the unique publications to come out of the American Civil War. Southern unionists—persons who remained loyal to the United States Government—existed in every Confederate state. Those unionists in the mountainous regions of the South, particularly eastern Tennessee and western North Carolina, have become well publicized. The same is not the case with the loyalists of Louisiana. Only the unionists of New Orleans and a few individuals from the states' country parishes have received the attention of scholars. To my knowledge, no one has ever cited Haynes's book in any study of Southern unionists, undoubtedly because of the obscurity of the publication.

Although Haynes's *Narrative* can in no way be considered a complete study of Louisiana unionists, it nevertheless represents an important source. Haynes's focus, as his title indicates, fell on western Louisiana. He barely mentions the pockets of loyal men and women in the Winn-Bienville-Jackson parishes area or in the region around Catahoula Lake, though he undoubtedly knew of their "sufferings." Also, because Haynes wrote a tale based upon his personal experiences, he did not record the story of those unionists (or anti-Confederates) in the eastern Florida parishes. Haynes stated in his introduction his purpose in publishing the book. By reprinting it in an edited form, I hope that it will truly, as he said, "contribute to the history of the great rebellion."

Haynes obviously published his *Narrative* not just to illustrate "the disposition of the people who originated, sustained, and controlled" the Confederate war effort and the "reign of terror." The return to political power of many of these men during the administration of Governor

James Madison Wells angered Haynes. This period of Confederate Reconstruction, as scholars have dubbed it, seemed to Haynes and other unionists a reversal of the results of the war. Haynes clearly stated in his subtitle that he felt Louisiana had not yet become fit for readmission to the Union. By publicizing his experiences, he undoubtedly hoped to convince President Andrew Johnson and the United States Congress on that point.

As one might expect from reading the book's title, Haynes expressed some harsh opinions about both Confederate soldiers and civilians who harassed and persecuted the unionists of northern Calcasieu, western Rapides, and southern Sabine parishes. His diatribe had a specific propaganda purpose, so it is decidedly one-sided. Loyal Confederates in the same area leveled similar charges of harassment, intimidation, and cruelty against Haynes and others whom they labeled Jayhawkers because of their armed resistance to Confederate authority. While I have verified most of the facts contained in Haynes's story, I cannot verify the base feelings and motives that he ascribes to his persecutors. I have avoided making value judgments for or against either them or the "martyrs of liberty."

Editing this book has proven both easy and frustratingly difficult. My interest in Louisiana Jayhawkers predated my discovery of the book, so I was already familiar with some of the sources that I used. Mrs. Jan Tate, whom I have found to be the most knowledgeable person on the subject of south Louisiana Jayhawkers, very kindly provided both assistance from her own research and encouragement in my pursuit of this editing job. Her input made the task much easier than it would have been otherwise.

The staffs of the following institutions were helpful in making available material in their collections: Louisiana and Lower Mississippi Valley Collection, Special Collections, Hill Memorial Library, Louisiana State University; Old Army Branch, National Archives and Records Service; Special Collections Division, Tulane University Library; Louisiana Adjutant General's Library, Jackson Barracks, New Orleans; and Louisiana Division, Louisiana State Library. My cousin,

Dr. Paul H. Bergeron, provided copies of documents pertaining to Haynes from those collected for the *Andrew Johnson Papers*, which he edited at the University of Tennessee.

A number of individuals contributed information used in editing Haynes's memoir. The following Haynes descendants provided encouragement as well as what they knew about their ancestor: Tommy Haynes of Robstown, Texas; Dorothy E. Phillips; Mrs. Mary B. Erickson of Grand Junction, Colorado; Julia Lee of Houston, Texas; and Steve Haynes of Grand Junction, Colorado. Sherry Bob Merritt of Snyder, Texas, and Francis Peveto Reid of Orange, Texas, graciously shared their research on Robert Washington Martin and John Peter Eddleman, respectively. Mary David Baker of Houston, Texas, and Constance D. "Petey" Birkholm of Solvang, California, assisted with sources on the Texada family. Greggory E. Davies of Winnfield, Louisiana, went out of his way to find records in the Winn Parish courthouse that related to Haynes's activities after the war.

My greatest difficulties came in tracing Haynes's biography and in identifying all of the persons he mentioned, particularly civilians. In some cases, names simply do not appear on census records, tax assessment rolls, or other official documents. In other instances, I could not identify a specific individual among a number of persons having the same surname. Few sources have come to light that contain biographical information on Haynes. Though I eventually succeeded in locating some of his descendants, they had few facts on his life to share. I welcome any information readers of this book can provide to clarify the omissions or mistakes I have made.

Arthur W. Bergeron Jr.

EDITOR'S INTRODUCTION

Dennis Edmond Haynes was born in Ireland, perhaps in Dublin, in 1819. Information provided by some of his descendants indicates that he and two brothers may have fled Ireland or England to immigrate to the United States. He probably reached this country in the early 1830s. He married Elizabeth Swearingen, who bore their oldest son in 1846 in Georgia. Haynes claimed to have served in one of the wars with the Seminole Indians in Florida. In 1850, he and his family lived in Lee County, Georgia. The census record of Haynes in that year gives his occupation as "grocerer." A newspaper account written during the Civil War states that he had been a lawyer in Georgia. His *Narrative* clearly marks him as a well-educated person. Haynes went to Nicaragua in the 1850s while the adventurer William Walker ruled that country. In Nicaragua, Haynes served first as a civil engineer and then as a topographical engineer for Walker's army.[1]

By 1858, Haynes had returned to the United States. Tracing his place of residence has proven somewhat confusing. In 1859, he received $110.68 from the Commissioners Court in Tyler County, Texas, for having taught school there, probably during the preceding year. Haynes appears to have moved his family to Rapides Parish, Louisiana, in 1860. They are listed on the census for that year, but the document does not give his occupation or any information on his wealth. Perhaps a neighbor provided the data in Haynes's absence. Haynes's wife and children also appear on the 1860 census for Tyler County, Texas, where she lived near several Swearingen families. Possibly Haynes was in the process of moving to Tyler County when the Rapides Parish census taker passed and had already sent his family ahead of him. When he enlisted in the United States army in 1864, Haynes gave his occupation as schoolteacher. He may also have run a farm in Texas and Louisiana. In a deposition given in 1873, Haynes stated that he had lived in Hardin County, Texas, from April 1, 1861, to May 21, 1863. He said that he "had a pre-emption of 160 acres of land" but had only "cultivated a garden on it." The editor has found nothing to substantiate this claim of residence in Hardin County.[2]

As talk of secession and war swept through Texas in 1860–1861, Haynes made no attempt to hide his strong allegiance to the Union. He claimed later that he had "exerted all my influence against secession." Haynes stated that he did not vote in the February 1861 election for representatives to the Texas secession convention "because it wasn't safe to do so" unless voting for a pro-secession candidate. He felt that his neighbors considered him an outlaw because of his unionist views. Haynes apparently suffered no retaliation and continued his livelihood for nearly two years. Perhaps encouraged by word of the formation of the First Texas (Union) Cavalry Regiment in New Orleans in late 1862, he attempted during the following spring to recruit a company of soldiers for the Union army, and the men appointed him as their captain. Before he could completely organize the company, Confederate troops moved to arrest Haynes and his men. Few men escaped, and Haynes found himself the object of a $500 reward.[3]

After several secret meetings in the swamps, the remaining unionists chose Haynes and a friend to go to Alexandria, Louisiana. They had learned that a large Federal land and naval force under Major General Nathaniel P. Banks had reached that town. Haynes and his comrade would tell Banks of their situation. They hoped also to persuade Banks to send troops on a quick raid into east Texas so that the loyalists and their families could be escorted to the army. Before the two men could reach Alexandria, they learned that the Federals had evacuated the town. Haynes decided to remain in western Rapides Parish rather than return to the Texas swamps or attempt to find his way through Confederate lines to a Union garrison. He lived for three weeks with an old friend from Georgia. Then he exchanged his Texas farm for one near the Calcasieu River, about thirty miles from Alexandria.

Banks's first Red River Campaign, as it is sometimes called, encouraged many Louisiana unionists openly to support the Federal army. Men from the piney woods hills of west-central Louisiana, as well as the swamps and prairies of south Louisiana, served briefly as scouts for Banks's troops. Others organized semi-military units that quickly became known as Jayhawkers. These men found themselves joined by Confederate deserters, draft dodgers, and even a few outlaws who wished either to assist the Federals or to impede the Confederate war effort. When Banks's army left the Red River Valley, Confederate troops, both regulars and home guards, began conducting active operations to break up the Jayhawker bands and punish the unionists who had provided supplies to the Federals. Thus began a three-month period that Haynes viewed as a reign of terror and called in his memoir the "massacre of the martyrs of liberty."

Haynes himself remained unmolested until October 1863. The man with whom he had exchanged land learned of his unionist sympathies and wrote about them to one of his former neighbors. This man revealed Haynes's secret to the commander of a Confederate unit stationed nearby. A cavalry squadron arrested Haynes and one of his sons and prepared to take Haynes to Shreveport, headquarters of the Confederate Trans-Mississippi Department. En route, he managed to escape, though he injured himself in the effort. Haynes attempted to get back to his home but fell into the hands of some home guards. One of them shot him as he attempted to get away. Turned over to another home guard unit, Haynes expected to be executed but again succeeded in sneaking away during the night. He made his way home and went into a swamp with his two eldest sons. There they remained in the home of a unionist for five days.

After a brief rest, Haynes decided to travel to Union lines. He went first toward Sabine Pass and then back toward south Louisiana. Confederate cavalrymen captured him near Franklin in January 1864, but he persuaded them that he was a loyal Confederate from Calcasieu Parish, so they released him. Haynes then struck out for Port Hudson on the Mississippi River and arrived there in late February. He took the oath of allegiance and obtained transportation to New Orleans. There he met with other refugees from Texas, including Brigadier General Andrew J. Hamilton, the Union military governor of that state. Haynes got letters of introduction from Hamilton and Louisiana's Union lieutenant governor, James Madison Wells. With these letters, he received permission to report to Union forces at Franklin so that he could report to their commander on the situation within Confederate lines. Haynes found in Franklin other unionists who were preparing to serve as scouts for the Federal troops.

The Union army began marching out of Franklin on March 14. General Banks was conducting his Red River Campaign and had Alexandria as his immediate objective. Haynes and the other scouts accompanied the lead cavalry brigade. Once the army reached Alexandria, dozens of loyalists (mostly Jayhawkers) began coming in from the swamps and piney woods to take the oath of allegiance. Banks authorized the recruitment of a regiment of cavalry scouts and gave Haynes and several others commissions to raise companies from their former neighborhoods. With about twenty men, Haynes went into the woods to look for recruits. He succeeded in enlisting more than one hundred men. On April 30, Haynes received an appointment as captain of Company B, First Louisiana Battalion Cavalry Scouts. The unit did little except drill and conduct scouting expeditions into the countryside south of Alexandria. Banks's Red River Campaign proved a dismal failure, and the scouts accompanied the army on its retreat from the town toward the Mississippi River.

Haynes's military service did not long survive the campaign. After an attack of typhoid fever and diarrhea, he went into a period of convalescence. He received a discharge by the War Department on July 16, 1864, because of his age. Haynes began seeking a means of supporting his family and applied for a political appointment. Governor James Madison Wells named Haynes as acting sheriff of Madison Parish on August 20, and he held that position until July 1865. He apparently returned to Rapides Parish because he later testified that he had acted as military postmaster at Pineville for the Union army. The chief quartermaster at Alexandria sent Haynes on some unspecified mission to Bienville Parish early in November 1865. He moved about November 8–10 to New Orleans. Haynes had found his home in the parish destroyed at the end of the war and had failed to secure legal redress against his "enemies" there. In late 1865 or early 1866, Haynes applied for an appointment as a federal surveyor at New Orleans. Although Governor Wells, Benjamin F. Flanders, Ulysses S. Grant, and Andrew Johnson recommended him, he did not get the job.[4]

In early December 1865, Haynes traveled to Washington, D.C. Alexander P. Field wrote Senator Henry L. Dawes that the visit came "at the instance of many Union men in this country to give evidence of the entire want of remorse [illegible word] amongst those who have been recently elected to all the offices in this state." Field went on to say, "The persecuting spirit of those lately in Rebellion, is worse now than it was in 1861." On January 30, 1866, Haynes testified before a subcommittee of the Joint Committee on Reconstruction. He remained in Washington and appears to have had a brief interview with President Johnson on February 8 at the recommendation of General Grant.[5]

Haynes's son Patrick had married in Tyler County, Texas, in March 1866, and he joined his son there sometime later that year. On December 23, Haynes married Permilia Dean. That marriage does not appear to have lasted long. The 1870 census for Winn Parish, Louisiana, shows him living there by himself with a local family. Permilia Dean remarried in Texas in late 1872. She was wed a third time, but apparently still remained in contact with Patrick, because she and her third husband sold him some land in Tyler County in 1883.[6]

By 1869, Haynes, son Patrick, and Patrick's family had moved to Winn Parish. At the time of the 1870 census, Haynes was living with farmer John M. Long, a native of Ohio and grandfather of future governor and United States senator Huey P. Long Jr. The census gave Haynes's occupation as schoolteacher. He purchased 40 acres of swampland along the Dugdemona River on July 19, 1871, but sold it to his son Patrick on July 11, 1872, for fifty dollars. Four years later, Patrick Haynes sold this parcel along with another 320 acres to John

Long and his son Huey for two hundred dollars. This relationship between Haynes and the Long family seems quite interesting. During the war, John Long supported the North but maintained an outward neutrality "for fear of reprisals" and because his wife's family "was sympathetic to the Confederacy."[7] Two of John's brothers were mustered into the Confederate army, probably as conscripts, but deserted soon afterward.

In April 1871, Haynes submitted a claim to the Southern Claims Commission asking reimbursement for animals he said he provided to some of his soldiers during the war. He stated that he had used twelve horses and two mules to mount men who had no animals of their own. When the army reached New Orleans after the Red River Campaign, Major Henry F. Williamson of the Second Louisiana Cavalry took the fourteen animals and refused either to return them to Haynes or pay for them. Haynes claimed that the government owed him $2,100. Several men, including former governor Wells and Haynes's son Patrick, testified in support of Haynes. The Southern Claims Commission denied the claim in 1874, basing its decision, at least in part, on statements that the animals belonged either to Confederate soldiers or civilians and that Haynes had captured them rather than having owned them. He had said he purchased the animals in Rapides Parish between March and May 1864, paying "for them in U. S. currency, and part in Confederate money." Haynes claimed that he kept them "on a small place I owned near Alexandria" until he took them into Alexandria for his soldiers to use.

Later, probably after 1880, the claim was referred to the U.S. Court of Claims, but surviving records do not indicate if this was done at the behest of Haynes or one of his descendants. This court also denied Haynes's claim. On June 26, 1886, it reported: "Under the circumstances it is not at all probable that he had any money to buy horses or any thing else, yet he claims that within a month he furnished these horses and mules to the Government. The only explanation of this sudden acquisition seems to be that he stole the stock or captured it from the enemy. We reject the claim on this presumption." Haynes's claim was transmitted on February 27, 1887, from the Committee on War Claims, House of Representatives, to the Honorable William A. Richardson, Chief Justice United States Court of Claims. The editor has found no further records of the case.[8]

Haynes became involved in local politics after moving to Winn Parish. In 1870, he became Superintendent of Registration and served as postmaster. The following year, Haynes became president of the Sub-Executive Committee of the Winn Parish Republican Party, as well as a parish school director. Haynes supported the Reconstruction policies of President Ulysses S. Grant and Governor Henry Clay Warmoth. On July 19, 1873, he received an appointment as district attorney pro-tem for Grant Parish. It is unclear whether or not Haynes ever assumed the duties of this office. He was in New Orleans on August 19 and gave his occupation as surveyor. Haynes disappeared from public records in 1873. The tax assessment rolls for Winn Parish in that year list him as a property owner.[9] He might have fled the area as a result of the hostile atmosphere in the area after the infamous Colfax Riot of April 1873. Some of his "enemies" were involved in that violence and certainly would have recognized Haynes if he were in the area. Efforts to locate information about him after 1873 have proven futile.

Tracing Haynes's descendants to ask them about the family's history has been somewhat frustrating. His children appear in a few records in Tyler County, but the editor has found no other information on most of them. Patrick and his family apparently left Winn Parish after he sold his land to the Longs in November 1876. He purchased land in Tyler County in 1880 and 1883. William bought one hundred acres there in 1873. Benjamin F., the youngest son, married in the county in 1872 and was involved in land transactions in 1875, 1876, and 1880. A female named Zelenor Haynes, who probably was Dennis's daughter and born in 1855, also married in the county in 1872.[10] Eventually, the editor succeeded in contacting several persons descended from Benjamin Haynes, but, unfortunately, they know little about Dennis before and after the Civil War.

A Thrilling Narrative of the Sufferings of Union Refugees, and the Massacre of the Martyrs of Liberty of Western Louisiana:

Together with a Brief Sketch of the Present Political Status of Louisiana, As to her Unfitness for Admission into the Union.

With Letters to the Governor of Louisiana and Noted Secessionists in That State, and a Letter to President Johnson on Reconstruction.

By Captain Dennis E. Haynes,
of the Louisiana Scouts.

Washington, D. C.:
McGill & Witherow, Printers and Stereotypers.

1866.

Introduction.

THE FOLLOWING NARRATIVE is that of a plain man telling his story in his own way; a simple record of his own sufferings and of other Union men in Western Louisiana and Eastern Texas, under the "Reign of Terror," during the rebellion. He lays no claim to scholarship, and he throws himself upon the indulgence of his readers for the errors in these pages, resulting from a defect of education. His sole object in this publication is to contribute to the history of the great rebellion some facts illustrative of its interior character, and of the disposition of the people who originated, sustained, and controlled it. He was an eye-witness in most of the transactions which he relates. For those sufferings he asks no sympathy. He feels sufficiently rewarded in the triumphs of the Government, and in the assured perpetuation of the Union.

The Author.

Chapter 1

*"I will deliver the plain unvarnished tale;
Nothing shall I extenuate, or aught set
down in malice."*

When General Banks whipped Dick Taylor on the Teche, in the spring of 1863, the Confederates broke, helter-skelter, in every direction; Taylor's army was demoralized. Had Banks followed up his success in that direction, he might have marched his army, with scarcely any opposition, to the Rio Grande; such was the terror struck into the Confederates west of the Mississippi, that they could offer no serious opposition to the advance of the Federal army.[1]

I was at that time living in Hardin county, Texas. Spaiths' [*sic*] battalion was ordered from Houston, Texas, to Louisiana, to reinforce Taylor. This battalion was chiefly composed of Texians from the southeastern counties.[2] Many of the soldiers deserted for their homes, intending to remain with their families at all hazards. Most of them were induced to enlist, at the breaking out of the war, by promises made to them by the planters, that if they would volunteer, their families should be supported. But, no sooner were the poor devils deluded from their homes, (afterwards to avoid being conscripted, as well as the prospect of their families being supported,) than the planters forgot their generous and patriotic promise, and, instead of assisting their families, extortioned on the soldiers' wives from one to three dollars a bushel for corn. Thus those cowardly vampires were fattening on the fat of the land, and enriching themselves on the misfortunes of their country and miseries of the poor. As a Confederate soldier's pay would not supply his family with cornbread, the soldiers' wives had to work in the fields like slaves, with their sucking babies laid on a quilt, under a shade in the field, whilst the mother plied her hoe to tend a patch of corn or sweet potatoes to keep them from starving. The piece of homespun, which they spun and wove, had often to be sold to the planter, to purchase a little corn for bread to keep themselves and children from suffering.

Knowing me to be an uncompromising Union man the deserters and conscripts sent for me, informing me of a meeting which they had appointed for all the Union men for the purpose of giving expression to their sentiments regarding the present state of affairs. The place of the meeting was a pond in the pine woods. We met, about fifty in number. I was appointed as one of the committee to draft resolutions expressive of the sense of the meeting, which was, briefly, their belief in the injustice of the rebellion and the incompetency of the Confederacy to gain its independence; that the rebellion was uncalled for by any act of the United States Congress, and much less by the election of Abraham Lincoln, and calling on the volunteers from the counties of Tyler and Hardin to return home, pledging themselves to suffer no conscript officer to take away any conscript or deserter; and, if any conscript or deserter should be spirited away, to fly to his rescue, and repel force with force, if necessary. Such is the substance of the resolutions which were unanimously adopted.[3] I, with a young man by the name of Phelps,[4] were appointed as delegates to canvass Hardin County, and call a meeting of the citizens at the Court House.[5] Whilst there, a traitor by the name of Joe Adams,[6] a one-handed man, who came to the meeting at the pond, and promised to render every assistance to the cause which he could, betrayed us. Whilst I was addressing the meeting at Harding [*sic*], my son came and informed me that I was betrayed; that General Van Vleek, a renegade Yankee from New York, of the militia,[7] had raised a company in my rear to capture Phelps and me. Our trial was over, our sentence passed; we were to be hung to the first tree which could be made to answer so noble a purpose. The evening before the meeting at Hardin Court House, the rebels of that county met at the appraisement of a dead man's property, and affirmed that if they could get ten men at the Court House they would hang me; but, such were the feelings of the people, as a general thing in that section of the country, in regard to the cause I had in hand, that they could not raise ten men in that county to molest me. Phelps and myself, seeing we were likely to be cut off from home, and being unarmed, took to the woods, and gathered round us such men as we knew we could depend upon in any emergency. We had several secret meetings in the swamps, and it was resolved that Phelps and myself should go to Alexandria to prevail, if possible, upon the Federal officers to give us a few squadrons of cavalry, and make a sudden dash into the interior, and bring out our friends. But, alas, we were doomed to a sad disappointment; for, before we got quite out of Texas, we learned, to our great mortification, that Banks had evacuated Alexandria, and before we got within sixty miles of Alexandria, we could distinctly hear the Federal cannon battering at Port Hudson.[8] We travelled all the way by night on foot, being compelled to leave our horses, to avoid detection; we traveled, in this way, one hundred miles in three nights; this was about the 20th of May, 1863. I would here remark, by the by, that the secesh had offered five hundred dollars reward for my capture.

We could neither advance nor retreat; we were between two fires; should we strive to get through the rebel lines, we would have to travel between two hundred and two hundred and fifty miles, and at every few miles would meet with some Confederate encampment; to return, we should have to remain in the swamps during the war, and if captured death was our penalty. A man by the name of Lazarus Goolsby,[9] a professor of religion, by the by, said he could see Haynes tied to a sapling and a pile of pine knots made round him, to which he would set fire, and freely do so, and turn his back and walk off laughing.

We came to a friend's house by the name of Henry Barrington,[10] an old friend of mine from Georgia, and stayed with him three weeks.

I had leisure to converse with many of my old acquaintances whom I met, having lived in Rapides parish about three years before, and, having learned the political sentiments of the people in that section of Louisiana, I made up my mind to remain somewhere in the neighborhood, and take advantage of circumstances as they might transpire. I therefore bought a place, with the crop, cattle, and hogs, from a man by the name of Presswood.[11] He was a great secessionist, and the Union men and him could not agree, so I sold him my place in Texas, stock and all. When I came to the Calcasieu I gave out that I was a good rebel. The Yellow-jacket battalion, under Major Fournett [*sic*], was camped at Hineston,[12] and the very day I came to the settlement they killed Jim Parker[13] on the public road, and shot perhaps twenty shots at his cousin Ben.[14] Parker was the first "martyr of liberty" in this section of Louisiana. It was but a few days afterwards that they killed Bob Flyn,[15] another Union man. They robbed and plundered the Union men of everything they could lay their hands on: horses, mules, oxen and cattle, wagons and harness, bed-clothes, plow-gear, horse bells, even the women's shoes and little trinkets of jewelry. The milch cows being too poor to eat, they caught the calves and yearlings, bored holes in their noses, and put a plow line through the incision thus made, and made them follow as docile as oxen. Major Fournett and his Yellow-jackets were as expert at plundering as Ali Baba and the forty thieves.

I would remark, in justification of the officers in command of the battalion, and especially of old Col. Fournett, who resigned in disgust at the orders issued to him by Gen. Mouton, which were "to burn all the houses of the Union men; to shoot every deserter they found with a gun; and any man they found out of his house after dark, to shoot or hang him within the following twenty-four hours."[16]

It is a fact worthy of note that the first robberies committed in this section of Louisiana, were committed by the rebels, which led to retaliation by some of the Union men, who, in return, robbed some of the rebels.

My brother-in-law brought me my family in August following,

and the day following he was captured as a conscript, by a squad of scouts from General Walker's division under a Captain Davis,[17] who came into the settlement hunting for conscripts. They camped at night on the Calcasieu river, at Strather's bridge. I prepared me some corn and a horse and cart to go to the mill, about twelve miles distant, but my real object was to let the conscripts know the cavalry was out. I saw about a dozen, and as soon as I told them the news they scattered in every direction to give the alarm. When I returned home, Captain Davis had my brother-in-law a prisoner, and several old men, whose sons were hid in the woods to avoid being conscripted. I went in search of Captain Davis; he was at the old man Wetherford's[18] house; Wetherford was a prisoner also; he was an old man sixty-six years of age, his head as white as snow; his offence was, his son was in the woods. I called Captain Davis out into the horse lot; told him I saw a dozen of "Jayhawkers" about twelve miles south of there, that a runner passed the day before, and crossed the Calcasieu river, about twelve miles south and spread the news. I told the captain that the "Jayhawkers" talked of fighting him; that I told them not to attempt it; "for," said I, "if you kill one of his men, he will bring the whole of Walker's division on you and kill every one of you he meets, and burn your houses;" that they finally consented not to fight him. Captain Davis swore that if they killed one of his men he would bring force enough to cut down every tree in the swamp and kill the last one of them. He said he knew who carried the news; that it was young Scarbrock,[19] whom he hunted out of his bed the night before. I found he was in Nicaragua with Walker,[20] and I being there too, turned the conversation in that direction; recited a poem I wrote on the siege of Granada, and before I conversed with him an hour he released my brother-in-law, and, further, gave me a certificate that he knew me to be a good citizen of the Southern Confederacy. He also gave me a written permission to harbor and protect Mrs. Mary Nichols, the widow of Simon Nichols,[21] (one of the rebels killed Nichols a few weeks before,) for they had interdicted any person from harboring her under penalty of burning their dwelling, &c. Had Captain Davis known the mission I was on, instead of the ostensible one of going to mill, he would have put a rope around my neck instead of giving me a certificate of protection.

Nothing of any consequence took place in the settlement except the robbing of a wagon belonging to some persons going to Texas. I did not know who did it, but suspected Dr. Dudley[22] and a Yankee deserter, who called himself Norton; but I learned afterwards his name was Green.[23] The rebel cavalry killed him in the prairies in 1864, but not before he killed two of them. I told the neighbors if this plundering was not put a stop to that evil would come of it; that the innocent would suffer for the sins of the wicked; and so, truly, it turned out. About the last of August Bob Martin, a quadroon Indian from Lana Cocoa prairie, Rapides parish, Louisiana, got a commission to raise a company of conscript hunters;[24] and he did hunt them with a mischief. So cruel and bloody was this wretch in his efforts to capture conscripts, murdering them indiscriminately whenever he found them, that he obtained the unenviable soubriquet of "Bloody Bob" Martin. It was on account of this inhuman wretch's bloody deeds that a foolish and wicked project was set on foot by some inconsiderate scapegraces—Levi Boyd, Wesley Lovin and Bryant Presley.[25] Martin and his company went home, and left at Martin's house several of their horses. These rascals induced several men and boys to go with them and kill "Bloody Bob" at his house. They raised a company of some dozen or so, and when they got to Martin's house, instead of attacking him, they took some horses out of his lot. Many of those inveigled into this trap, finding out the real object of the expedition, returned home, and would have nothing to do with it. "Bloody Bob," next morning, finding the horses missing, started on their track, and finding the course they went, mustered his company, and compelled all he met to go with him. Bill Smart, and his brothers Dr. Smart and Reese Smart,[26] with a mulatto by the name of Jim Groves[27] for his first lieutenant, and Big George W. Smith[28] for his second lieutenant, also joined him. (Smith had, a few days ago, been appointed constable by Governor Wells, Oct., 1865.)[29] Smart and his company came to the house of an old man named Walley;[30] he found in his pasture a horse which they recognized as having been stolen from "Bloody Bob's" lot. Walley's son-in-law, Lovin,[31] put the horse in the pasture. They found another man, a conscript, in Walley's house; him they shot dead, and Walley they took about half a mile from the house, and hung the old man from a tree till he was dead. There was not an honester or more inoffensive man in the country than this poor man. The next house they came to they shot two more men; one being shot in the bowels, cried out with pain. Reese Smart jumped from his horse and pulled out his bowie-knife, cursed him for a damned Tory, and stabbed the already dying man in several places till he was literally butchered in the most cruel and barbarous manner. Next day they caught two men on the road, one by the name of Clark[32] and the other Elijah Connelly.[33] Clark being a conscript, and upon being questioned if he would tell the truth they would not hurt him, he told them he was one who was decoyed to "Bloody Bob's;" that he never went to the house; had nothing to do with stealing the horses; told the names of several who were along. His confession did not avail him; they broke their promise, and when about to shoot him he begged for heaven's sake to let him go and see his children, (six in number.) But no; no respite was given him. Connelly would have made his escape but for his cousin. His name was Bass.[34] Bass was the only man who saw him pass a mound in the woods. He rode after him and brought him back. Connelly was on foot. This wretch told—and Connelly did not deny it—that he passed himself on Connelly as a Union man. Connelly thought he was all right; he being his cousin had no idea that he would lie to him, much less betray him. Bass told that about three weeks before Connelly told him he went from Rapides parish to Natchitoches parish to let the conscripts know the cavalry were out conscript-hunting. This Connelly did not deny, and they shot him dead, and left him and Clark to be devoured by the vultures. The same party visited Governor Wells' summer-seat,[35] and took or destroyed everything that they could find, and finally burned the whole establishment. They robbed and plundered the Union men everywhere they went, and under the ostensible pretense of suppressing robbery and jayhawking, before the close of the expedition they robbed and out-jayhawked the worst jayhawkers in the country. And whilst I am treating of the stealing—if it can be called stealing to steal from such a pack of ruffians as "Bloody Bob" and his company—not one of the scamps who got up the expedition was captured.

I would say here, in connection with the foregoing narrative, that the Union men, to show that they did not countenance any lawless deeds, raised a company of their own and went to scour the country of jayhawkers. But when they saw the lawlessness of the very men who were denouncing robbers, murdering and robbing indiscriminately, they withdrew, and as soon as they dispersed "Bloody Bob" and his conscript hunters were at their heels.

Captain Todd, another conscript hunter, was at the same time operating between the Calcasieu river and Opelousas. He surrendered himself to Banks' army at Natchitoches in April, 1864, and went to New Orleans. He is now a land office agent at Opelousas, and was, I understand, appointed through the influence of Governor Wells.[36] This is strange indeed; but he is not the only one in the list of exceptions to the governor's favors. That Governor Wells should recommend such a man as Todd as a proper recipient of Government favor could be scarcely believed, were it not for the fact that, while reorganizing the State of Louisiana, he (the governor) appointed to the highest offices in the parishes men whom he knew to be notorious rebels, while it was a rare instance that he ever appointed a good Union man to office.[37]

Chapter 2

*"Then, as a terror to the following age,
Like Badjazet, I'll bind him in a cage."*

I WAS LEFT in comparative quietness till Presswood, when he got to Texas, wrote back to one of his friends, Jake Gunter,[1] the ruffian who, after taking the oath of allegiance at Alexandria in 1864, went back and joined the rebels, and, from his local knowledge of the swamps, was one of the leading conscript hunters up to the time of the surrender. It was he who shot the notorious Dr. Dudley.[2] Gunter told the rebels I had had to leave Texas; that I was outlawed there for raising a company of Union men, five hundred dollars reward being offered for my apprehension. I was now suspected strongly of being a Union man, and I had to have recourse to Captain Davis' certificate, and other papers which I brought from Texas, to keep me from being captured. But the cat leaped out of the wallet at last, for a renegade Yankee by the name of Jones,[3] from Woodville, Tyler county, Texas, being a captain in the Confederate army, on his way through the settlement reported me to Major Pat. Keary's battalion, which was then camped at Hineston, eight miles from my house.[4] They sent a squadron of cavalry to capture me, with several of the neighboring rebels for guides. I was, with my two little sons, in the horse lot, attending to some fattening hogs, when the cavalry charged upon the house. I could have easily escaped had I known their object was to take me a prisoner. I went to the house and met them in the yard, when a sergeant asked me if my name was Haynes. I told him yes. He told me I was wanted in Hineston and had to go. They also took my oldest son,[5] though I showed them the record of his age; he would not be eighteen years till the coming January. I did not know what charge they had against me till one of them, a sergeant, a Mason, told me I was arrested for being a Union man in Texas.

At this time Pat. Keary, a planter, and his two brothers were moving their negroes and stock to Texas.[6] His train covered over a mile of the road. He stopped at Hineston several days for his teams to come up. He had a pack of bloodhounds along, trained on purpose for running negroes. If it had not been for them I should have made my escape from Hineston. I sent for my wife. She came, and went to Mrs. Keary and begged her to intercede with her husband, the major, to release me. Nothing could be done in my behalf. Mrs. Keary told her that she did her best, but that the orders were from General Dick Taylor to kill every man that did not come in.

The Yankee renegade, Captain Jones, came with Keary to the guardhouse and identified me; telling Keary in my hearing that he knew me well in Texas; that I was a shrewd fellow, &c. Finding all hopes of escape cut off on account of the bloodhounds, and three other prisoners being brought in, Keary ordered a double guard to be placed round the guardhouse. Knowing Keary when I lived in Rapides parish, about three years before, that he was a Mason, and also Jones to be one, and finding all entreaties vain, I expected nothing but to be shot; and so I learned afterwards was their intention. As Keary and Jones left the guardhouse I called out, "Major!" Both turned round. I was standing in the door of the guardhouse, and gave them the masonic sign of distress. Not long afterwards an orderly came and asked me my Christian name in full, which I gave him. I then believed I was safe, and that, instead of killing me, I would be sent to headquarters; which was the case. The three prisoners who were brought in the night before were, on the following morning, tied with their hands behind their backs with rawhide strings, their spurs and knives taken from them, and sent under guard to "Bloody Bob" Martin, and, as the sergeant who had command of the guard told me afterwards at Manny [*sic*], Sabine parish, were shot to death.

I was captured on the last Saturday in October, 1863,[7] and about the middle of the following week the battalion took up the line of march for Shreveport, to which place they were ordered to carry me to General Kirby Smith,[8] under a charge of high treason. The guard who had me in charge had orders to tie me on my horse. One of them led my horse by the bridle, riding by my side. My son they turned loose when they left Hineston, no charges being preferred against him and he being under conscript age. He was, however, recaptured and sent to "Bloody Bob" Martin to Lana Cocoa prairie, and every means but torture used to scare him, to get him to join them, without avail. They finally turned him loose, and he had to walk home—about fifty miles.

The first night we camped at a free negro's by the name of Carrol Jones.[9] I was, after supper, tied, and a double guard placed over me. Keary's train camped there too.[10] He had along all his stock, cattle, and sheep, about twenty wagons, about a dozen carriages, and three hundred negroes, three or four of whom were handcuffed and tied together with a log-chain, and a negro guard over them with old muskets and bayonets. Here I should have tried to escape were it not for the dogs which were along. We finally reached Manny, after a march of three or four days—which could be easily accomplished in two days; but Keary's property had to be guarded, lest the "Jayhawkers," as they called all the Union men, might pounce upon him and capture his negroes and concubines.

When we arrived at Manny I was put into the jail, and in the jail was an iron cage seven feet by five; and in that cage I was thrust, in company with a Creole Frenchman from Avoyles [*sic*] parish and a negro. The officer of the guard was a nephew to Keary, and a greater brute I have never come across. I asked him to take the negro out of the cage the following morning. He told me he would not. I sent word to the captain in command that the cage was too small to hold three men, that one was a negro, and that, if he had no respect for me, to have some respect for his color, and have the negro taken out of the cage; which request he politely granted. I should give his name here if I could recollect it. The name of the lieutenant of the guard, Keary's nephew, is Patrick Loftus.[11]

I will here, by the way, state a conversation I had with Keary's nephew, Lieutenant Loftus. When he opened the cage to put me into it I asked him why he was putting me into such a place, and with what crime I was charged to merit such treatment as to put me in a cage, like a wild beast, in company with a filthy runaway negro. He answered he had orders to put me in close confinement. I asked him with what offence I was charged. He told me high treason. I denied having ever committed any; that I owed no allegiance to the Confederacy; that I was an adopted citizen, and had taken the oath of allegiance to the United States Government; that I was a Union man, and should never deny it; that I could not commit any political act which could be considered, justly, more than that of a belligerent, and consequently I should not be charged with anything more, and should be held only as a prisoner of war; that I could not be considered a spy, having lived in the Southern States twenty-five years before secession; that all that could be said against me was that I denounced the conscript act, and the exemption in that act of all persons owning twenty negroes or five hundred head of cattle from military duty in the Confederate army. He answered that, seeing from my conversation I was a man of education, he was astonished at my making use of such language; that he knew of several men being shot for speaking against the exemption in the conscript act. Then said I: "What are you fighting for?" He answered, "Liberty." "Liberty!" says I; "to hell with such liberty where a man is shot for criticising [*sic*] on an act of congress; I don't want such liberty." I would here remark that Major Keary's father and mother were Irish born, and his nephew, the aforesaid Lieutenant Loftus, is an Irishman. I have seen it verified in many instances, especially during the brief reign of Knownothingism,[12] that the worst enemy an Irishman had was an Irishman's son. It is so even in the animal kingdom, for the worst enemy a wolf has is his bastard son, the wolf-dog.

We stayed in Manny seven days, waiting for Keary's cavalcade to pass us on its way to Texas. The battalion then took up its line of march to Shreveport. They had five prisoners along of their own men. One was a sergeant by the name of Lee,[13] from the parish of Avoyles, who, should he be alive and see this narrative, can vouch for its accuracy. I was ordered by my Irish lieutenant friend to dismount and let Lee ride. I felt unwell, and being otherwise afflicted, I did not feel able to walk. He cried out in a rage, "Don't you tell me you won't do anything!" I had to dismount; but in a short time I got upon my horse behind Lee, and while I rode behind him we concocted our plans of escape, resolving not to go to Shrevesport [*sic*] if we saw any possible chance of escaping. I told him that many of the company were good Union men, and had told me if at any time they were placed over me as guards by night to run off into the bushes; that they would fire off their guns, but I need not be afraid of getting hurt. The first night after leaving Manny we camped at an abandoned plantation late in the evening. The weather was very dry, and water scarce. The prisoners were put in an old smokehouse. Some of the men were very hungry, and after preparing their supper I induced the orderlies of three companies to get me supper. I had more than enough, which I prudently divided with two of the guard, one of which tied my horse to the back of the old smokehouse and the other got him some corn. We now set our wits to work to plan for our escape, the men being very busy preparing supper; some hauling corn and others cutting up a couple of beeves before the smokehouse door and dividing it to the different messes. The battalion was composed principally of backwoods Americans, Creoles, Frenchmen, Spaniards, half-breed Indians, &c.; so they kept up a jargon, "every nation in his own tongue." While the soldiers were busy in dissecting the beef, we were as busy in digging a hole with my knife under the logs. There was a sentry sitting at the door, and eight more of the guard lay down before the door. While Lee was digging I lay with my eyes open, watching, but feigning to be asleep. I snored away with all my might. The sentry got to nodding about the time Lee finished digging. He got out of the aperture with much trouble and noise, and took the knife with him to cut loose a horse to ride. I being a larger bodied man than Lee, was held bound by the log, the hole he dug being most too small to admit of my escape. I had no knife to make it larger, and every minute was an hour to me; so I made one bold push, and in doing so I got through, but with my breast bone broken. I led my horse to a clump of trees in the edge of the field and near the fence, where Lee was to go out and wait for me. I did not see him. I whistled for him three or four times, but he did not answer, nor have I seen him since. This was between ten and eleven o'clock at night of the 3d of November, 1863.

I had neither bridle nor saddle; I used a rope line for a bridle, and two blankets for a saddle. I took a circuit round the camp; the moon was past the first quarter, but it turned cloudy, and sometimes I could not see the moon nor stars. I struck for a southeast course to avoid the town of Manny, because I knew a squadron of the battalion remained there to pick up any stragglers who might be inclined to drop back. I kept the woods and by-roads, crossed several plantations, until next morning, when I struck a road which was much traveled. It being cloudy I could not see the sun, and did not know where the road led to. I tied my horse to graze and watched the road; saw carriages and horsemen travel both ways, but I was no wiser than before of my exact locality. I finally resolved to go to the house, get my horse fed, and make inquiries. I saw a white boy in the yard, about seventeen or eighteen years of age, and my first question was, to inquire how far it was to Manny; he answered eighteen miles. This gave me encouragement; I asked him what road this was. He said it was the road from Natchitoches to Shrevesport, and that it was twenty-five miles to Natchitoches. I felt comparatively safe, as I was out of the track which the remainder of the battalion would have to take from Manny to Shrevesport. His father came to the gate; I told him I wanted breakfast, and my horse fed; told him I was lost; that a squad of the "Black French" took my bridle and saddle from me the evening before; that, upon my complaining of this ill treatment, they threatened to take my horse; that I learned from their conversation, there were more behind them; that I took the first left hand by-road I met to avoid the rear guard, and got lost; that I lived near Spanish lake, northwest of Shrevesport, and was going to see my brother-in-law, who lived on the Calcasieu river. My tale was swallowed whole, for some of the same battalion were in the neighborhood the week before and took a fine horse from one of his neighbors; but, upon his reporting the case to Gen. Smith, he got his horse back. He went with me three miles of the way; saw a Confederate captain and the man whose horse was taken the week before. He told them, briefly, how I was treated; they gave me directions how to take by-roads to go to the Calcasieu river. Every place I stopped I told the same tale in order to account for my riding barebacked, and with a rope bridle. I got along finely until the afternoon of the next day; I got a bad scare, for, as I rose a hillock in the pine woods, right before me on a trail, within two hundred yards, was a squad of cavalry riding towards me. My hair stood on ends; I thought it was "Bloody Bob" and his cursed crew. Making a virtue of necessity, I put on a bold face and rode on. I gave them the road, bowed, and saluted them politely. I do not know whether they observed my accoutrements or not; they passed on without asking me any questions, for which I was more than ordinarily thankful. I learned that night they were a squad of the Natchitoches conscript hunters. My grey beard was my protection from interruption.

That night I rode by torchlight till I got to a Union man's house, and, having informed him who I was, he treated me very kindly. Next day I took by-roads and sometimes rode through the woods. In the evening I struck one of the roads leading from Texas to Alexandria; I left the road to my left and struck through the woods. When I struck the public road again I thought I was at old Clark's old field, from where ran an old road to a friend's house. I entered the old field, but could find no road. I rode all round the plantation, when I saw a man riding a horse and leading another. I hailed him; he stopped and turned back; I asked him whose place it was; he answered, "Archie Smith's."[14] "Then," said I, "I know where I am. I was lost; I thought it was old Clark's." I let down the fence and got out; he waited for me. He was a

Creole Frenchman by the name of Vansaux;[15] we rode up to Smith's gate; Smith was in the yard. Vansaux said, "Mr. Smith, here is a man I found in your field." I said, "No, you did not; I hailed you and asked you whose place it was." He said, "Yes." Smith hollooed to his wife, "Bring me my double-barreled gun! bring me my double-barreled gun!!" very much alarmed. I started to ride off. Vansaux haulted [*sic*] me and pointed at me a Derringer pistol, and ordered me to halt a second time. I said, "What shall I halt for? you have no right to stop me on the public road." Smith kept hollooing to his wife for his double-barreled gun. I believe they aimed at killing me, for Smith knew me, and was one of the men who piloted Keary's company of cavalry to my house when I was first captured. I thought, therefore, I would risk the pistol before the double-barreled gun; and as Smith's wife did not bring the gun as quickly as Smith wished, I set spurs to my horse as Vansaux presented the pistol at me a second time, swearing he would shoot me. I was looking at the muzzle of the pistol, and, as he shot, I saw the fire roll out of it; the horse being tired, having rode about seventy-five miles in little over a day and a half, and being in company with other horses, refused to answer to the spur. As Vansaux fired I threw myself a little on my left side, to dodge the bullet as the horse started, and if he had answered to the spur I would have dodged it. I fell off the horse, but caught on my feet, not feeling in the least hurt. I ran for a creek swamp about two hundred yards distant. When they saw me running, they became furious, thinking Vansaux missed me; they set Smith's dogs on me, and, as I ran, I found my right arm swinging and my hand slapping me in the face, and the dogs tearing my legs. Vansaux overtook me on horseback, with Smith's gun, and carried me back to the house. Upon examination I found my right arm broken about three inches below the shoulder joint, as I threw myself on my left side when Vansaux shot, my right arm being extended horizontally; the ball, breaking the bone, traversed along the shoulder joint and lodged in the cartilage which connects the shoulder with the breast, where it remains to this day. Smith and his wife bound up my arm the best they could; and when Smith saw I was entirely unarmed he appeared very sorry for what he had done. I must say, in justice to Mrs. Smith, that were it not for her I should have been shot to death; for, as Smith acknowledged, if his wife had handed him the gun when he called for it he would have put two loads of buckshot in my back as I ran toward the swamp. This took place on Saturday afternoon, on the 7th of November, 1863, eight miles west of Hineston and forty-three miles from Alexandria, Louisiana.

CHAPTER 3

"Thou shalt behold him stretched in all
the agonies
Of a tormenting and shameful death,
His bleeding bowels and his broken limbs
Insulted o'er by a vile, butchering villain."

WHEN MAJOR KEARY first came to Hineston, he established what he called a "home guard." He sent out squads of cavalry and brought in every man and boy who was capable of bearing arms, and many who were too old to bear arms, under the ostensible purpose of protecting the country from the "Jayhawkers." He placed a man over them as captain by the name of Ivey.[1] Ivey was a low-bred, petty grog-shop gambler, and as mean a wretch as ever disgraced human nature. "Bloody Bob" Martin was a gentleman, compared to Ivey, as the sequel in this narrative will show. This fellow, with his company of "home guards," was stationed at Hineston. Smith and Vansaux forced me to go with them to Hineston, and so alarmed were they lest I might be rescued from them by the Union men that they whipped my horse to make him keep pace with them, though I was now realizing keenly the effects of my wounded arm and broken breast bone, and by the time we got to Hineston I was swollen from my breast to my back bone, the bandages being tied on when wounded. My arm swelled, and I was in the most excruciating agony. Here an underhanded game was playing without my knowledge. It was proposed by some of the company to kill me right off. I had a great many Union friends in the company, who, by way of intercession, stated that it was not necessary to kill me then; that I would die anyhow. Others were lukewarm, or, through fear, were not willing to have my blood upon their hands; so that, when a vote was taken, only six voted for me to be shot. These were Ike Swett, a mulatto free negro, — Taylor, the two brothers Hop and John Swan, — Graham, and a young Roussou.[2] Ivey, finding his company would not kill me, wrote to "Bloody Bob" to come from Lana Cocoa to kill me; that he could do nothing with me with his company; and that I was not able to bear the journey, being too badly wounded. One of my friends stood behind Ivey while he was writing the letter, and told me next morning to get away if I could, and pointed toward the place where there were no guards stationed.

Next morning I got a friend to let my wife know the state of affairs, and tell her to come to see me and bring the children (six in number) along. She was sick, and, being naturally delicately constituted, the news of my late misfortunes only served to render the state of her health more precarious. Mrs. Nichols, of whom I spoke in the first chapter of this narrative, and living with my wife, brought, in an ox wagon, the five youngest; the oldest boy being afraid if he went they would keep him a prisoner also. She brought me bed clothes and some food to nourish me. I told Mrs. Nichols I was not as bad off as I made it appear; that I was severely wounded and in great pain, it was true, but that my health was good; and if "Bloody Bob" did not come in a few days and kill me, the Union men would assist me to escape; also to tell old lady Boyd, whose three sons were in the woods from the beginning of the war,[3] to have a horse ready every night; that if I effected my escape I would call on her on my way home. This plan was arranged between the two ladies. On Sunday evening one of "Bloody Bob's" men came to Hineston and told the guard in my hearing that Bob Martin would be certain to be in Hineston on the following day; that he started with a part of his company that morning from Lana Cocoa. I now saw I was on the eve of life or death, for if Martin came he would show me no mercy.

That night two men were placed as guards over me, both to guard and wait on me; and that night I was resolved, upon any reasonable chance presenting itself, to effect my escape. One of my friendly guards, when his turn came to watch and nurse me, laid down by the fire at my feet and fell fast asleep, as did his comrade also; previous to this I told them I surely had to go out in the night, and had them to put on my shoes and lace them tightly, and fix my blanket over my shoulders. I then laid down, or rather had to be laid down, for I was quite or nearly helpless. About ten o'clock all the company, as well as my guards, were fast asleep, as I judged from the quiet which reigned in the camp. I made three efforts to get up, but failed; I thought of Robert Bruce and the spider,[4] and renewed my efforts, though with great pain; with God's help I succeeded, the fourth effort I made, to get in a sitting posture, and being strong in my extremities I got on my knees; laying my left hand upon a bench near me I stood upright, lifted the latch of the door and walked out. It being a fine, clear moonlight night I looked around, and seeing no person stirring, walked slowly (I could not move fast) towards the Calcasieu river swamp, through an old field, and struck the Texas road from Alexandria about six hundred yards from the guardhouse. It was three miles to Mrs. Boyd's, and in traveling through the swamp I had to go a new-cut road, full of stumps and roots. If I had had the misfortune to have fallen down, I do not think I could have risen again; but Providence favored me, and I got safely to the old lady's house. She was true to her engagement; she had her old riding horse ready in the lot, and her two daughters lifted me on the old horse. Next morning the young women took my back track from their home to the swamp and put out my tracks, the roads being very dry and dusty. If the rebels knew of their aiding me in escaping they would burn their house; which, by the way, was afterwards burned by the bloody wretches, Martin and Ivey, after Banks evacuated Alexandria in 1864.

I got home safe and turned the old horse loose, lest any person should be seen carrying him home. My wife, upon seeing me return once more alive, rallied from her sickness, which was more the effect of her bereavement upon my account than from any constitutional malady. I changed my bloody clothes, and a little before day went into the swamp, with my two little sons to nurse me. Early next morning a squad of fifteen men, with a lieutenant, one Matthew Lynch,[5] came to my house looking for me; as a matter of course nobody had seen me; they inquired for my sons; they were told they had gone to Texas. Lynch started on the Texas road inquiring for them. Next day the search was made with more men; the swamp was scoured; one of my camping places was found, and an empty milk bottle; this encouraged them to a more minute and extended search; but every night I moved my camp, and lay up during the day in the cane and undergrowth, whilst my boys kept a good lookout; not a bird or squirrel could hop on a limb without their hearing it. My enemies put out an order—Ivey and "Bloody Bob"—that whenever we were caught there we should be shot. My Union friends would send my wife word of everything that passed, and one of my boys would steal up to my house to get provisions and learn the news. I told the boys, in case we should be surprised, to get away the best way they could, and leave me to my fate.

The fourth day after my escape my friends sent my wife word that a hundred men were to hunt for me, and that I had better move further from home. We accordingly started for the "Bay," a large swamp which ran parallel with the Calcasieu river, and from one to two miles distant. I could travel but slowly; one of the boys carried the bed clothes, and the other, provisions. It was twenty-five miles to the "Bay;" we traveled by night, and laid up in the swamp by day. On the ninth day after being shot, I got to a Union man's house by the name of Cloud. The rebels afterwards killed one of his brothers, and hung his father, an old man upwards of seventy years of age,[6] for carrying provisions to his sons in the swamp. My arm had not been dressed since I was shot. Cloud and myself and my boys, and some more Union men who were at his house, went into the river swamp to dress my arm. The stays and bandages which bound my arm were so glued together from the blood and corruption as they coagulated, that the bandages had to be cut off with a knife; the corruption, when at liberty to flow, ran in a stream to the ground, and under my arm there was a tablespoon of worms. In fact, I stunk like carrion.

I was now informed that I had better not go in the "Bay," as most of the neighbors here had joined Ivey's company, and they knew every foot of the camping ground from being in the swamp themselves; and the weather being so dry, very little water was to be had there but from stagnated pools, and they would be sure to hunt for me about the water-courses. So I went into the river swamp; it was here so thick with cane and undergrowth, that a man could hardly be seen ten feet distant. Here I was in comparative safety; but another difficulty presented itself. The Union men who lived here had been so harassed for the last two years by the rebels, that they raised nothing but a few potatoes, which their wives cultivated. When my little stock of provisions, which my boys brought with them, failed, I could get nothing to eat but a few sweet potatoes, and not many of them; these were my only food for the last five days I remained in this neighborhood.

I learned from the Clouds that the home guard found that I had quit the neighborhood in which I lived, and were coming to hunt me where I now stayed; so I left for home, traveling by night and laying up in the swamps by day. On the morning of the sixteenth day after being shot, I got home—not to the house, but near it. I got clean clothes, and plenty of good nourishment, and, instead of going into the big swamp, camped on a little creek about a mile from home, believing they would hunt for me in the large swamp and overlook the little creek, which was the case. On one occasion while there, it rained all night and the next day, and as my camp was composed of a few poles, and covered with but a single quilt, I sent the boys home to sleep in the fodder house. My wife was uneasy, and would not let the boys stay, but sent them back; her prudence here, I believe, saved my life, for about half an hour before they returned my arm got to paining me to such a degree that I thought I could not live till morning. I had the boys to unloose the bandages and take off the stays, upon which my arm run black blood to at least a pint; when it quit running the pain ceased.

At this time all but very few of the Union men joined Ivey's company to keep from being torn up. I could scarcely trust anybody. He issued an order that no person should go to my house or do anything for my wife. My faithful Mrs. Nichols—I learn she is now dead—Ivey put in the guardhouse; but I still had friends left in spite of him. A young man by the name of Levi Pedro,[7] a paroled soldier from Port Hudson, and his brother-in-law, by the name of Johnson,[8] though in Ivey's company, would go to my house by night and kill her a hog, and cut her wood, and do many things for her. Also, a widow Bass[9] would send her daughter across the swamp, and carry her meal, and take her foul linen under her saddle as saddle-cloths, to wash, and bring them back in a loose sack under her riding skirt. Pedro joined the Louisiana scouts, and is now, I learn, in Illinois.

I was now mending fast, and could travel comparatively well, when my friend Rollin Wetherford sent his daughter to my wife to let her know that two hundred men (Ivey and "Bloody Bob's" companies) were to hunt every hole and corner for me the day following. This was the twenty-third day after being shot. So, about two hours before day on a frosty Sunday morning, 29th of November, we started to Sugartown, about thirty miles southwest, on the road to Nibblet's Bluff, Texas. At sunrise I got to old John Doyle's, a free negro.[10] I went in to warm. One of his sons, belonging to the "home guard," was at home. I had no fears of them, but they had of me, so strictly and severely this wretch punished any person who disobeyed his orders; and his lieutenants, the Swans, were equally as bad as he. I sat by the fire to warm. There was a pot of cornmeal coffee boiling, and I longed to get a cup even of this; but the old jade, instead of giving me a cup of coffee, told me I had better leave, as they were looking for some of the company every moment, going that way to Hineston. I left, and about a mile from the house I quit the road and laid in the woods all day, it freezing all the time. The boys could jump and dance, (we dare not make a fire, lest the smoke would attract attention,) while I had to lay on my back. Sometimes one of the boys would sit on my feet to keep me from freezing. Before sundown we started, and traveled about five miles. This was but a settlement road; I dared not travel the public or military road. I knew the road forked somewhere not far from where I had now got to. We were now warm from traveling, and, being tired, we laid down till the moon rose, so we would not miss our way, and when we woke up we were almost frozen. The moon having risen, we started on our journey. It was very cold; it was the coldest winter, in this latitude, I have known for twenty-five years. When we came to Six Mile creek it had to be crossed on a small cypress foot-log. Here was a hard case for me; hardly able to travel on level land, how was I to cross the creek on a foot-log? My boys' hands were almost frozen; it was with great difficulty they could cut me a hand-pole with a dull knife. They had then to steady me on the log, I having but one hand to use, and the log bobbing up and down. If I should fall in, I should be either drowned or frozen to death; but God was with me, for I crossed the frail bridge in safety; and, after crossing two more creeks on foot-logs, but more firm, I got to a friend's house—a cousin to my wife—about three hours before day. I woke them up; they got us breakfast, and, after being well warmed, we laid down on a comfortable pallet near the fire. The madam washed my coat; it was covered with the corruption that ran from my arm.

The next morning I started again, leaving my youngest son here. I got by the following evening to my old friend Barrington's. He and his son had gone to Texas, to keep from being conscripted, under the ostensible excuse of purchasing beeves for the Confederate army. I would here remark, by the way, that a scoundrel from Sandersville, Rapides parish, Nat. Sanders[11] by name, and his son, were with the two Barringtons in Texas, upon the same business, and, after getting back, Sanders joined "Bloody Bob's" company and hunted the Barringtons. The elder Barrington was taken sick in the swamp, and went home and died. Two days afterwards they captured his son, and it was left to this wretch (Sanders) to say whether he should be killed or not, as he was with him in Texas; so, after a short consultation with the officers, young Barrington was tied to a tree and shot dead.

> "Butchers and villains, bloody cannibals,
> How sweet a plant have you untimely cropped!"

The Barringtons were originally from Twiggs county, Georgia. After killing young Barrington, they heard of his father's death; and, to be certain that he was dead, they went to his house, and swore that if he was not dead they would "dead" him.

Whilst at Barrington's I sent for my old friend, Dr. Farquahar.[12] The doctor and his family were from Ohio. He came to see me. He told me of his being captured by the rebels, and his son also. The son they put in the army; but he stayed but a few days, when he made his escape. Himself they were going to kill, and had their guns presented at his breast. General Walker being present, he asked the general what charges were against him, more than that he was a Union man; that he was a Northern man by birth; that if they killed every man who was a Union man for merely being a Union man, he thought the Confederacy must beat a low ebb. General Walker saw nothing against him to warrant his being put to death, and immediately ordered his release.

I now consulted with the doctor as to what course I had better pursue, which way I had better take; that there was no chance for me to remain in this section of the country, crippled as I was. He advised me to go to Captain Carrier[13] [*sic*], near Opelousas; that he had upwards of fifty true men with him, and that he would, no doubt, send me to some of his French friends, where I would be taken care of till I got able to travel; to come to his house the following night, and he would have a horse, and go with me some distance. I here left my oldest boy to take care of himself; and as the rebels knew the Barringtons were gone to Texas, it was not likely they would call that way, as it was a mile from the public road.

I went to the doctor's next night; he was waiting for me. I got on the horse, and he walked ahead, leading the horse by the bridle. We had not got three-quarters of a mile when, close by a rebel's house, the horse stumbled, and, being tender in the mouth, jerked the bridle out of his hand, and so unable was I to ride that the horse threw me, and, unfortunately, I fell on my broken arm. The pain was so acute I could not help crying out with some woeful exclamations; but the poor doctor was as badly scared as I was hurt. He mildly informed me that Iles[14] was a rebel, and there might be rebels at his house, who, if they heard any noise, might come out and capture me. I was as quiet as a lamb, despite my agony, and laid down by a tree; the horse ran home; the doctor followed him, and brought him back, with another gentle old horse for me to ride. We now got on the horses, and went along very well, about four miles, till we got to a friend's house by the name of Pollard.[15] Pollard was not at home; he was a conscript, and in the swamp. The doctor examined my arm, to see if it was rebroken; but it was not; but it swelled up, apparently double its former size. Mrs. Pollard had me a comfortable feather bed made down by the fire, and had me a cup of Confederate coffee made early next morning before I started.

I would here remark, with regard to the members of this family, there were Pollard's wife, and his brother's widow and children, and four orphan children—in all ten children. Pollard joined my company, and went with me to New Orleans—when General Banks left the Red river—where he died at the barrack's [*sic*] hospital. Here was a distressed family, having nothing to support them.

Next morning at daybreak I started on foot, weak and sick enough with pain from the fall, from the house where I was, to get to a Union man's house, by the name of Green Pharris.[16] I walked on the grass, lest my tracks would betray me; and so weak was I that I thought I could never get there. It took me four hours to travel four miles. When I got to Pharris' he was not at home. I told his wife who I was; and, knowing me from character, she was glad to see me. She had no meat; but she killed me a chicken, and made me nice soup. She dressed my arm; the blood and matter had run down to my shoes—the fall from the horse making it bleed afresh. I laid on the bed to rest, and about an hour by sun her sister came, and said that a part of Ivey's company were at her house and captured her husband, Paul Young.[17] Here was cause for fresh alarm. Not long afterwards Pharris came home, badly scared, confirming the news of Lieutenant Swan being in the neighborhood, and that it was dangerous for me to remain at his house—as he was a conscript it was very probable they might come to capture him—and advised me to go to the old man Burt's;[18] he was over age, and it was very likely they would not go to his house, as they had not as yet even called there. In going to Burt's I had to cross a large creek; but the foot-log was in proportion to the creek, and flattened on the top side. I got over without any difficulty. It was dark when I got to Burt's; but I had no difficulty in the way of entertainment. These poor people, as soon as I would tell them my name, knew me at once, my misfortunes and persecutions having been the theme of sympathy since I was captured. I told Burt that Pharris, as was agreed upon, was to be at his house before day, and take me to the conscript's camp, on the Big Whiskychitta creek.[19] That night there were four or five guns fired off at the "cavalry" camp, and Pharris, being somewhat of a timid nature, got scared, and, instead of calling for me, broke to a creek swamp, six miles from home. Burt, finding that Pharris did not come, and hearing the guns, went to see what became of Pharris; but finding him gone he, too, caught the contagion of alarm, and at break of day woke me, saying, with considerable agitation, "Mr. Haynes, you are in danger." He then informed me of the guns being fired off, of Pharris' alarm, and that the "cavalry" was camped but four miles from his house.

I now had to diverge from my direct course. Burt went with me about a mile and a half, to show me the way where I had to cross the Whiskychitta creek. It was a bad prospect for me, sure enough; the creek was about sixty feet wide, and eight or ten feet deep—the foot-log a sweet gum, blown up by the roots from the opposite bank, and full of limbs. Burt could not walk a log but on "all fours." I tied my saddle-bags round my neck, to have the use of my left hand to hold to the limbs—my blanket round my shoulders blowing by the wind, and catching to the limbs of the foot-log. But I could not swim; so, if I had fallen in the creek, the weight of the saddle-bags round my neck and the blanket as an incumbrance, I should certainly have been drowned. But a kind Providence, in whom I put my trust, carried me over safely. Not far, within sight, was a house at which I was to call, to put me on the trail that led to a good Union man's house, by the name of Jones,[20] and from thence to old Billy Simmons'.[21]

Here, as I came through the field within plain view of the house,

I had a new but (as it turned out) unnecessary alarm. I saw two horses saddled in the yard, and several men in the gallery looking very earnestly toward me. My broken-arm coat sleeve being sewed up and my blanket over my shoulders, I put on a bold face, making a virtue of necessity, for if they were enemies it was too late to retreat. So I walked up boldly and saluted them. I do not know who were the most alarmed, they or I. Upon a close examination I discovered two or three budgets lying on the gallery. One of the men began to question me pretty closely, to know where I was going and what my business was; and, seeing their anxiety about my business, and that their baggage did not correspond with soldiers' baggage, I remarked that it looked like, from their budgets, they were inhabitants of the woods. My loquacious friend answered, smilingly: "It does look so." I then informed them that they had better look sharp; that the "cavalry" was on the other side of the creek the previous evening, and captured Paul Young. This made them open their eyes, for two of the four were Young's brothers. They had came from near Opelousas, and were going home; so they concluded to return down the creek to a camp where there were some more conscripts. I told them my way laid in that course and I would go with them, whispering to the spokesman that among women and children I did not wish to make myself known, but would tell them who I was as I went along. One of the Youngs gave me his horse to ride, and when I told them who I was they were ready to do anything for me—nay, die in my defence. I rode with Young about seven miles, till I came to Big Whiskychitta creek. Young went down the creek, crossed on a foot-log, came up on the other side to where a canoe was tied, and ferried me over. I laid on my back in the little boat lest I might fall overboard. It was but about three-quarters of a mile to old Billy Simmons' house. I walked up to the fence and called the old man out. I briefly told him who I was, and asked if he had heard of the "cavalry" being out. He knew me by reputation, and was glad to see me. He and his wife, during the three days I stayed with them, nursed me as if I was one of their own sons. Finding his house was on the mail route to Opelousas, and some Texian soldiers having called there, I was apprehensive, and so was he, that it would not be a safe place for me to stay any longer, though, from my wound, over anxiety for my safety, and weariness, I felt very weak.

He saddled a couple of horses, and rode with me himself to within a mile of Carrier's ferry, on the Calcasieu river. The bridge over a little creek within a mile of Carrier's being broken, the horses could not cross. The old man fixed me a foot-log to cross dry-footed. He then bade me God-speed and returned home.

The old man Carrier[22] was a Creole Frenchman, and neither he nor any of his family could speak English. He was not at home when I got to his house; but a man by the name of Beyham,[23] who lived a few miles from there, and who could speak both French and English, happened to be at Carrier's when I got there. I told him my name; he knew me well though he had never seen me before. It was but a short time before this that the "cavalry" had him a prisoner, and made him dig his grave. I do not recollect now how he made out to get away. When the old man Carrier came, Beyham told him who I was. The old man was glad to see me, but, his house being upon the public road, and the "cavalry" having his ferry as a regular crossing place, he thought it would be a bad place for me to stay. He then was informed that I only wanted to stay till morning, and, if he could not carry me to a friend's house about eleven miles further on, that I wanted to get to his brother's, Captain Carrier. The old gentleman and his lady took good care of me, had my arm dressed, and gave me one of the best beds in the house to sleep on. Next morning he took me in his buggy to his friend's house, eleven miles on the road to Opelousas. I am sorry I have forgotten this man's name.

I was now finally exhausted, and could travel no further; I remained with this good man seven days. He nursed me like a brother, for which I shall forever feel thankful. He also sent his little son with me on horseback across the prairie, it being impassable on foot, and afterwards I traveled three miles till I came to a Creole Frenchman's house, to whom I was directed. He was a paroled soldier from Vicksburg, but swore he would not go to fight any more. He took me in his tilbury, about five miles, across another prairie. I walked two miles to another Union man's house, where I stayed all night. Here, while he was dressing my arm, a piece of bone came out of the wound. He next day carried me in his buggy about six miles. I was now within five miles of Captain Carrier's; but I lost my way in the Bayou Mallet swamp, and could not find the bridge nor a foot-log; till, tired from looking for one, I saw a log reaching across the creek, about six inches under water. I with much difficulty cut a little sapling to answer for a set-pole, and with equal difficulty took off my shoes and socks, tied my saddle-bags round my neck, and slid down the bank the best way I could to the foot-log. I got over safely, my chief difficulty being in putting on my shoes and socks, for it hurt me to stoop, my breast bone hurting me as well as my arm. Seeing an opening I made towards it, and struck the public road to Opelousas. I inquired at the first house I came to for Captain Carrier's residence, and after getting directions where to leave the Opelousas road, I again made inquiries. Here I was questioned very closely by every man who could talk English, and, after much difficulty—in having to cross the Bayou Mallet a second time, and in finding the Catholic church where I was told I should find the captain's domicil—when I got there I could get no direct information. None of the women of whom I made inquiry could speak English; here I was in a quandry [*sic*], till two men, quadroons, rode up, one of whom could speak pretty good English. After satisfying themselves that I was all right—for, as he said, they were looking for an old man who was wounded in the arm—he informed me of the exact locality of Captain Carrier, and volunteered his services to carry me to where he lived. I was now again exhausted and could go no further; but he said it was only a mile and a half, and to get behind him on his horse, which I did. He however did not take me to the captain, but to a house where three men were secreted, who, to my joy and their's also, were the three brothers Boyds, and sons to the old lady who furnished me the horse the night I made my escape from Hineston. They were truly glad to see me, and as I was, excepting my wounds, in excellent health and as hungry as a wolf, the boys prepared me supper, which consisted of corn bread, sweet potatoes, fresh pork, and Confederate coffee; to all of which I did ample justice.

Next day I saw Captain Carrier. He is a pure-blooded Creole Frenchman; speaks no language but broken French; had he had a good education he might have been a man of note, and made his mark in the world; but, unfortunately for himself, he is quite illiterate. I next day went to an old quadroon lady's house, where the captain boarded, and stayed with her about two weeks. My arm now began to heal, but I could not move my hand as yet. I went back to the Boyds', and we lived together for about ten days. During this time my oldest son came to me; he was afraid he would be captured. There were a thousand and one rumors of the "Yankees" coming up to Washington and other places, and we were kept in a continual state of excitement, not knowing what to do. I told my son to get himself some employment where he would be safe, and I would run the risk and try to get to the Federal army; but how to get there was a question easier asked than answered. I had but $30 in Confederate money, and no horse; the distance to New Iberia, where the Federal army was stationed,[24] being upwards of eighty miles; the prairies knee-deep in water, and the roads ditto in mud, brought to my memory the exclamation of King Richard the Third after the battle of Hastings—"A horse! a horse! my kingdom for a horse!"

Chapter 4

"A prison is a house of care,
A place where none can thrive,
A touchstone true to try a friend,
A grave for one alive;
Sometimes a place of right,
Sometimes a place of wrong,
Sometimes a place of rogues and thieves,
And honest men among."

I FINALLY OBTAINED from a quadroon a poor prairie pony, which he had taken up somewhere; he was very poor, and hardly able to carry me. I got a pair of old plow bits and a piece of raw cowhide, of which the Boyds made me a bridle, and in lieu of a saddle had a corn sack stuffed with moss strapped on the pony's back with rawhide thongs, and straps of the same material for stirrups. I now hired a free negro to pilot me to the Yankee lines for $30 in Confederate money. He could not speak a word of English, nor could I speak French; so we rode along like two dummies, and traveled all night; it was cold and freezing, and by an hour after sunrise we got, about half way to New Iberia, to a friend's house (a quadroon.) My Rosanante gave out, and so did

I, for I was taken with a violent cold, and laid up three days; during which time I learned to my great mortification that the Federal army had moved to Franklin, twenty-eight miles down the Teche from New Iberia.[1] I now swapped horses with my guide; he was to go with me to Franklin, but he only went with me till I got on the public road on the east side of the Teche, then left me, keeping the $30. I rode along, and at St. Martinsville had to swim my pony, the bridge being burned. I went to a negro's house who kept a kind of tavern, and learned from him the situation of affairs in general. I was afraid to trust my secret to any white person, there being a squadron of rebel cavalry camped near St. Martinsville. Learning from citizens, whom I heard conversing about the Yankees, that the small-pox had been in New Iberia, and that they left a doctor and nurses there to tend the sick, and having found the locality of the hospital, I resolved the next night to leave the pony with the old negro, and travel on foot nine miles. I set out after dark, sometimes through the plantations and sometimes on the road. I was taken very sick again, and laid down several times to rest. I got to New Iberia about eleven o'clock at night; and seeing the light in the hospital I knocked at the hall door, and was answered by a soldier of the 114th New York infantry, who was one of the nurses. I told him what was the matter, and wished to see the doctor. My reason for wishing to stay in the hospital being, that there was no chance of detection unless I should be betrayed; I did not dread the infectious disease, having been inoculated with the small-pox when a youth, and knowing the Southerners all dread the small-pox as much as a Northern man would the yellow fever, and as none were allowed to leave the hospital but the doctor and the nurses; and as the doctor was a Federal officer, and the nurses Federal soldiers, I thought myself safe enough till the following night, when I intended to start for Franklin, by a "flank movement," through the prairie by the rebel pickets, which were stationed along the public road which ran from New Iberia to Franklin. But I calculated without my host, for I was basely betrayed by the Federal doctor.

When I got to the hospital the nurses informed me that the doctor had gone down to the Yankee picket lines, and would not return till some time next day. The nurses were two Irishmen; one's name was McCormick.[2] They took a lively interest in me when I related, briefly, a part of the troubles I had encountered. About three o'clock in the afternoon the doctor came to the hospital, and seemed somewhat surprised to see me there, with my arm in a sling. I briefly told him what my business was, and, as a matter of course, he being a Federal officer, I acquainted him with the main particulars of my case. He said: "This is no place for you to be. Have you been vaccinated?" I answered: "No; but I have been inoculated, and I only wish to stay for protection till night." This was the substance of our conversation. He left me. I would have staked my life on his fidelity; but, alas! I was doomed to a sad disappointment. The doctor's name was Hubbard, and he was assistant surgeon to a Zouave regiment from New York.[3]

About four o'clock in the afternoon of the 16th of January, 1864, McCormick, one of the nurses, came into the room where I was. He looked as pale as death. I knew something unpleasant had happened before he spoke a word. His first words were: "You are betrayed; here come six of the devils, with their carbines, right for the hospital." And, sure enough, they were coming. Some went round the house, while the sergeant in front demanded of the nurses to bring out that man who was wounded! Seeing all hopes of escape cut off, I went out, and was greeted with a salutation that was anything but pleasant or gentlemanly. They ordered me to march ahead of them, cursing and damning me as we went. One offered me fifty dollars if I would run. They would ask me desultory questions, and, as I would be about to reply, they would curse me and push me along with the butts of their guns. I saw my two poor Irishmen walk along on the opposite side of the street. They looked the picture of despair; for, as they afterwards told me, they expected me to be shot every moment.

They now brought me to their headquarters, which was in a deserted livery stable, and I was confronted by their commander, Major J. D. Blair, of the 2d Louisiana (rebel) cavalry.[4] A Captain Stafford,[5] from Rapides parish, was also present. I was now subjected to a strict examination, mental and bodily, for the traitorous doctor informed them of my arm being broken, and, in substance, of everything I told him. I was ordered to strip off my clothes, so they might examine my wounds; having bound my arm with woolen bandages to keep out the cold, and it being tedious to unloose them, the gallant major ordered them to be torn off, which was done with as little ceremony as if I had been a brute instead of a human being.

When asked how I came to get my arm broken, though I despise from my soul any prevarication from truth, yet the desperate situation in which I found myself placed made me make statements which were not in accordance with truth, in order to save my life. I stated in general terms that my arm was broken in an affray; that my coming to New Iberia was in search of a daughter whose husband was killed at the siege of Port Hudson; that when last she wrote me she was at St. Martinsville; that I was informed at the latter place that she came to New Iberia as a laundress to some Federal officers; that the cause of my going into the hospital was, that I could see no light in any house but at the hospital, and, being sick, (which was a fact,) I called to get some medicine. My going into the Yankee hospital, they said, instead of coming to their quarters, laid me liable to a strong suspicion of my not being all right. I declared (which was a truth) that I did not know they were encamped in town, as a Confederate soldier told me the day before that they were encamped further down toward the Federal pickets. My name, I told them, was John O'Brien, and that I lived in the Sugartown district of Calcasieu parish.[6] I had the precaution to place my residence in a district where I knew the inhabitants, expecting that men were there in the different regiments from almost every section of the country; what I suspected proved to be a fact, as they asked me if I knew any persons there, and, if so, to name them; upon which I readily gave the names of Dr. Farquaher, the Iles, the Johnsons, &c.[7] This satisfied them that thus far I told the truth; but it bore against me, from the fact that the Sugartown district were mostly all Union men, or, as the rebels called them, "Jayhawkers." I was searched for papers, but none were found upon my person to give any clue to who I really was. They put a guard over me, and, having but a light, single blanket, and the night piercing cold, with the soft side of a rough plank for my bed, I suffered severely; having also a bad cold, which was the occasion of spitting blood all the night and next day, and great pain, which I incurred from the rough manner in which they made an *ante mortem* examination of my fractured limb.

Next morning, before I got anything to eat, I was ordered to get ready to march. A piece of corn bread and fresh beef were thrust into my hand, and I was told to get into a little wagon which was passing. I did so as soon as I could, for I was unable to travel on foot a single mile. The provost marshal of Vermillionville and his guard escorted me to the town. I was placed in the sheriff's office, in the court house, in which the provost guard had a pile of corn, and a guard placed over me. Here I underwent another examination by Lieutenant Whitaker,[8] the provost marshal; but, as I gave the same answers here to similar questions as those propounded to me at New Iberia, my name was placed upon the guard book as "John O'Brien, of Calcasieu parish, arrested by Major J. D. Blair, 2d Louisiana cavalry, at New Iberia," and charged with being a suspicious character.

I was now for the third time cribbed, if not caged; and if no person came who should identify me, I hoped to be able to effect my escape, or get discharged in a short time. So I formed to myself a line of policy not to give the least possible suspicion of my having any idea to make my escape; and I gave out that, as I was captured without a just cause, neither would I leave without being honorably discharged.

Sooner than expected, I had an opportunity of proving to the provost marshal my sincerity of the foregoing statement. Having slept but very little at New Iberia, and being weary from my ride in a rough traveling vehicle, I coiled myself on the pile of corn, and fell fast asleep. When I awoke my guard was fast asleep, too, and snoring away. I now determined on my escape, and to make for Vermilion [*sic*] bayou, and, if I could find no means of crossing otherwise, to swim over the best I could with one arm. The chance for escape seemed so favorable, that I sat right up and put my blanket over my shoulders—when I was doomed to another bitter disappointment.

Just as I was about to walk out—for the door was not locked nor the windows fastened—I heard the heavy tramp of a pair of boots in the passage, which proved to be the provost marshal, coming to visit the guard. Seeing my hopes of escape cut off this time, I thought I would make a virtue of necessity, and prove very conclusively to the provost marshal my being entirely innocent of being any such a person as a "suspicious character." As he took hold of the knob of the door-latch, I took an ear of corn in my left hand, and, as the provost marshal opened the door, struck the sentry with it, and woke him as the lieutenant entered, he seeing the ear of corn fall on the floor. He gave the sentry one of the devil's blessings, remarking, "that man might have made his escape, if he had a mind to." I replied I did not intend to leave, unless honorably discharged, as I had been arrested without any just cause. "I believe it; I believe it," he replied, "and I shall do everything I can for you."

I was the only prisoner they had, with the exception of a little Englishman who deserted from the Federals; but I was not long so, for in a few days they brought to jail a young man charged as being a guide to the Federals when Banks drove Taylor from the Teche; and the day following they brought in old Judge Belden,[9] whom they sent, in a day or two afterwards, to Alexandria. In the course of a week the room was crowded with prisoners under different charges; some as being spies, some for desertion, and some as conscripts. The sheriff's office not being a secure place of confinement, the jail, being very foul, was now cleaned out, and the prisoners were ordered into it. I had been, in the meantime, very sick, and had to have a doctor to visit me. I was treated very scientifically, and soon got better; but my fare, for a sick man, was very coarse and indifferent. I was not put into the jail-house with the others for a few days during my convalescence. I was at liberty to walk all over the court-house and yard, but slept in the jail at night, except the first. I might have made my escape unperceived, but I did not feel well enough to travel, and having secured the interest of the provost marshal, by my apparent disinterestedness, I hoped in a few days to be released. After being confined here about two weeks, three Federal prisoners were brought in, and they, with others charged with crimes, were sent to headquarters at Alexandria. This gave me hopes of my being shortly set at liberty, for if I had been charged with any heinous offence I would have been packed off there too.

After being thus confined for twenty-eight days I was, to my great joy, informed that Col. Vincent[10] had ordered my release, at the special and frequent solicitations of Lieutenant Whitaker, the provost marshal. More especially, as the lieutenant informed me, he had written to the enrolling officer of Calcasieu parish to know if there were any charges against "John O'Brien" of that parish. The enrolling officer wrote back that "John O'Brien" was a loyal citizen. I was informed afterwards at New Orleans, by a refugee by the name of Smith,[11] that there lived at that time in Calcasieu parish a man by the name of John O'Brien, who was a good rebel; so they turned me out of jail as being the Simon-pure "John O'Brien" of Calcasieu parish, the provost marshal giving me a passport to my home there.[12] So I bid them goodbye, regretting I could not travel any further in that direction in search of my fictitious daughter.

During my confinement in this filthy prison, I had been literally covered with vermin. There was scarcely the breadth of the palm of my hand on which there was not a scab, and on some parts a dozen, having to tear my flesh, from the itch occasioned by these noxious vermin. I had been six weeks without a change of linen, having but two shirts and very light clothing; I had, to keep from suffering from cold, to wear them both at once. I tried several times at Vermillionville to get one washed, but could not.

CHAPTER 5

"I'll read you matter deep and dangerous,
As full of peril and advent'rous spirit,
As to o'er-walk a current, roaring loud,
On the unsteadfast footing of a spear."

DURING MY CONFINEMENT in Vermillionville, I became acquainted with an Irish conscript, belonging to Captain Schemell's company, 2d Louisiana (rebel) cavalry,[1] who had been under arrest and confinement forty days, for not reporting in due time after being exchanged; he was captured, or rather got himself captured, at New Iberia, by getting drunk, in order, as he told me, to give the Yankees a chance to capture him. He was from Morganzia [*sic*], Louisiana. He gave me a way bill to Port Hudson, and told me where the rebel pickets were stationed. I made the best of my way back, fifteen miles northwest of Opelousas, where my oldest son was concealed with the Union Creole French. I then put a suit of his clothes on, and had my filthy ones washed, and two days afterwards started on foot for Port Hudson. I heard of a good Union man by the name of Fitch[2] living in Washington, on the Bayou Cortabla [*sic*]. When I got to his house he was not at home; his wife, upon informing her of my business, kindly received me into her house, and kept me all night.

I tried to get on board of a flat-boat to go down the bayou to the Atchafalaya river, but I was informed by a Frenchman, a Union man, that Dick Taylor would allow no cotton to be shipped from there by private individuals; that all the cotton shipped was "government" cotton; that a Captain Lyon[3] was hired by "Little Dick" to purchase cotton for him, to be delivered at the mouth of the Cortabla, at fifty cents, Confederate money; that "Little Dick's" brother-in-law was then delivering the cotton to merchants from Illinois, who were paying for it in gold and silver.

On the morning of the 16th of February, 1864, I left Washington for Port Hudson. It snowed pretty much all day. In the height of the snow storm I left the town unperceived, and traveled under the ostensible purpose of looking out for a school. I had to be very cautious in making my inquiries, and had, without any particular desire on my part, to make the acquaintance of notorious rebels, the better to effect my real design, to secure me from suspicion.

One morning I took breakfast with one of this class; he was the most hot-headed fire-eater I had met with. I humored the old fanatic to his heart's content; sung him a rebel song, cursing the "damned Yankees" in general, and the abolitionists in particular; eat [*sic*] a good warm breakfast, "free gratis," and departed, with many a hearty good wish for my success and prosperity. I next called, at the suggestion of my host, on a member of the rebel legislature, which sat at Shrevesport, who had the day before returned home, to make inquiries whether the legislature had made any provisions for free schools, &c.; and after a half hour's conversation with him on the state of affairs in general, and of schools in particular, I left him, he directing me to call upon Colonel Ash;[4] that a teacher was wanted in his settlement. I did call, or rather had to call, lest my not doing so might create suspicion. The colonel was not at home; his house was presided over by an elder brother, who was a cripple, having lost a leg. They were at dinner when I called, and when they got through they invited me to the table, which invitation I gladly accepted. After telling my business I found they had a school in full blast, which I was heartily glad to hear, though apparently very sorry for my disappointment. To turn the subject from myself and the school business, seeing they were of the aristocracy, and to flatter them all I could without their being aware of the true cause for my doing so, I asked the old gentleman whether he was in lineal descent connected with the Ashes of Cape Fear, North Carolina, of Revolutionary memory? He replied that Colonel Ashe of Cape Fear was his uncle or granduncle, or some near relative, I do not remember which. I then made a draft on my Revolutionary lore for the incidents connected with Colonel Ashe and Governor Martin, of North Carolina, and after displaying my pedantry by eulogizing the valor and patriotism of the Ashes in general, and of his honored kinsman in particular, I left the house, with all the school business information they could give me, and their hearty good wishes for my success.

The weather continued very cold for this latitude; it snowed, and the earth froze. I came to an old gentleman's house; he was out on the roadside. I asked him if there was a house a couple of miles ahead on the road, where I could stay all night. He answered "None, except that of some colored people." I told him I did not wish to put up at such places if I could help myself. He invited me to stay with him; that I was welcome, if I could put up with such fare as he had. I gladly accepted his hospitality, especially as it was getting toward the cool of the evening, and I being thinly clad. He treated me very kindly, and, as I professed to be a good rebel, I passed the night till bedtime in cheerful converse "on the state of the nation." The war was the chief subject of conversation, and as a gentleman and his daughter from Washington happened to drop in soon after my arrival, the merits and demerits of the belligerents were discussed with kind good humor, especially as all of us were, for the time being at least, of the same politics. The madam took occasion to remark that Lincoln was the best president we ever had; that he made all the women of the South industrious; "God bless his soul, I hope he may be hanged; ha, ha, ha." We all, as a matter of course, joined in the laugh, and before retiring the "Throne of Mercy" was invoked for innumerable blessings to be poured out on the holy cause of the Confederacy.

On the following morning, February 19, the ground was frozen; hot water had to be poured on the faucets of the cistern to get water.

I started on my way towards Port Hudson. I learned from some colored men, who kept a blacksmith shop, that a rebel picket was at Peek's ferry, on the Atchafalaya river,[5] and that no person would be let pass who had not good papers, or whom Peek would not recommend. It was seventeen miles from where the roads forked to Morgan's ferry, and ten miles through the swamp. When I got to the forks of the road, I made inquiries of a blacksmith, who kept a shop there, what the prospect was of getting a school on the other side of the river, about Bayou Fordoche. He told me I need not go there for that purpose, that the citizens had nearly all abandoned the county. So I dropped my character as schoolmaster, and assumed that of a gardener. I traveled through the swamp, sometimes knee-deep in mud and water, for a quarter of a mile at a time. I thought several times my toes would freeze, and at several sloughs I had to strip and wade; this took me a long time to get through the swamp. When I got to the river I found Morgan's ferry was broken up, but I was informed a mile further down, that I could cross at Mr. Burton's.[6] He had a kind of boat—half ferry and half batteau. I called at the house, and the old gentleman came out; he was a venerable looking man, with a countenance denoting intelligence and good nature. I anticipated having some difficulty in getting put over the river. I told him my business; that I wanted to cross the river to go over on the Fordoche, and having a staff in my hand about four feet long, I presented myself before him as a decrepit old man; for, from my then forlorn appearance and gray beard, I passed for being ten years older than I really was, and, as I before remarked, having changed my ostensible profession from a pedagogue to a horticulturist, I put on my broadest Irish brogue, so it would be hard to tell but that I had just vegitated [*sic*] from the Emerald Isle. The old gentleman told me that he had orders from the military to put no one over that he did not know, or was not recommended to him. I told him had I known that, (naming the old gentleman with whom I stayed the night before,) that he would have given me a "bit of paper" to him, but he did not tell me that I would have any trouble in crossing the river; and I wound up by saying that I did not see why anybody could object to crossing such a poor old man as I was. He then replied, "Well, I don't think so either." So, calling a couple of the "boys," he told them to put me over; the ferriage for a footman being $2, Confederate money. As the negroes were ferrying me over, I made inquiries of them if any Confederates were stationed in the neighborhood. They informed me that there was a picket at Catlin's[7] house on Bayou Fordoche, which was five miles from the ferry; and they gave me particular directions how I should know when I came within half a mile of the place, by the number of bridges on the road, and of a plantation, and a right-hand road. I understood the topography of the country from my knowledge of its geography, and when I came to the forks of the road I made another "flank movement," which was nearly as hard upon me as the swamp I had just crossed. I took through the woods and old fields, through brush and brier, water and mire, for about three miles. I had sometimes to stop fifteen minutes at a time to pick off the cockle burs which stuck to my clothes. I at last struck the Fordoche, by following an old trail, at a foot-log; the moon was past the first quarter, and shone all night. I had not tasted food since sunrise, and being compelled to keep my broken arm in my coat sleeve, to avoid detection, I suffered a great deal of pain from my fractured limb. I surrounded every house on the road till past bedtime, lest I might be challenged and taken up again as a "suspicious character." About eleven o'clock at night I saw a light in a negro's cabin; I went up and peeped through the logs of the hut, making no noise till I found who its occupants were. I found a negro in bed, with his hand badly cut by being caught in a gin stand while ginning cotton, and a woman sitting up with him. I could trust the blacks, knowing well their feelings about the war, so I asked them if they saw any rebels about. They informed me that that same evening a great many passed up, and were staying about two miles back the road I had come. They were at a house at one side of the bayou, and I passed on the other; here was a narrow escape. The negroes told me they traveled in a hurry; that they had a fight the day before with a Yankee picket on the Gross [*sic*] Tete bayou. Being very hungry, I asked them for something to eat; I got a piece of corn bread and a joint of the backbone of a shoat. I devoured it in a hurry, and left the vicinity, not choosing to make any further acquaintance with the "chivalry" than I could possibly help.

I had not traveled a mile when I heard a noise as if it were a carriage of some sort, and, hiding in the bushes by the roadside till it passed, I saw it was a negro driving an ox-cart. I traveled a little further, and, keeping in the shade of the timber, I could see a person a good way off without being seen myself, the moon shining brightly, and it freezing. I observed a man walking toward me. Concealing myself in the bushes till he came opposite me, I discovered he was a stalwart negro, and, having no fear as regards this "species of chattel," I made myself known to him, and briefly told him where I was going. He gave me directions how to go to False river, and told me when I got to where the Fordoche ran into Gross Tete bayou to take to the left, cross a bridge, and I need not be afraid of meeting any rebels on the route; so, if I got two miles further without meeting an enemy, I would be out of danger. He had with him a pint bottle of Louisiana rum, and he gave me a couple of drinks, which I needed very much, as I was greatly exhausted. I met with no difficulty till about two hours before day, when I came to a bayou which ran into Gross Tete bayou. Not finding either bridge or boat, I called at a house, though very loth [*sic*] to do so, and made inquiry how to cross. The man was a Dutchman, and spoke such broken English that I could hardly understand him, and in trying to follow his directions I got into the woods. I had to return the way I went, and wake him up again. He then went with me to the bayou, where he had a boat, and ferried me over. I had no more difficulty in finding the way till I got to a large plantation on False river, about ten miles from Port Hudson. I called at the house and asked the servant if I could get breakfast. She went up stairs and made the inquiry, and the answer which she brought me was, "Massa will be down directly." "Massa" came down in about a half hour; a tall, gaunt, grisly-looking personage of the "lousy aristocracy." He questioned me rather impertinently, which I suppose he thought my uncouth appearance warranted him to do; and, maintaining my character as a gardener, I did not disabuse him of the apparent contempt I saw he viewed me with. His name was Hebert.[8] He asked me where I was from, where I was going, and what occupation I followed; and I had to answer his several inquiries before he would tell me whether or no he would let me have my breakfast. I told him I was from the Fordoche, that I was looking for work, and that I was a gardener. After an hour or so breakfast was ready. I saw a lady as if in the act of coming down stairs, but she, getting a glimpse of me, saw directly by my habiliments that I was not a fit person to sit at the same table with her ladyship. She, no doubt, was too much of an aristocrat to be seen at table with a plebian.

I left my host to think what he pleased about me, and bent my course to Port Hudson, the goal of my safety. It was about one o'clock p.m. when I got opposite Port Hudson, tired and weary.[9] My energies seemed to flag as I drew near on the opposite bank of the river; but when I saw the brave old flag, the "Stars and Stripes," floating over what the rebels once thought "impregnable Port Hudson," my heart expanded with joy at beholding the good old flag I had not seen for years, and to get within the protection of whose folds I had endured so many hardships and passed through so many dangers. When I got to Port Hudson I had, in a little over a day and a night, traveled fifty-two miles on one meal.

Chapter 6

"I pray, sir, deal with me in misery
Like one that may himself be miserable;
Insult not too much upon my wretchedness,
The noble minds still will not when they can."

I HERE SUBSCRIBED to the "Iron-clad," and got transportation to New Orleans. I was anxious to get to Franklin and inform the commanding officer there of the "situation" in his front. When I got to New Orleans, I saw in the morning paper an account of a meeting of the Texas refugees and a synopsis of the speech of General A. J. Hamilton, military governor of Texas.[1] I found him at the City Hotel, and on presenting him my card he looked at me and inquired: "Are you the man?" I was a woful [*sic*] looking specimen of humanity—

"My hat with half the crown beat in,
My trowserloons not worth a pin,
My coat deficient of a skirt,
And with, at best, but half a shirt."

The general asked me, "Are you without means?" I answered, truly, "I have not a cent in the world." He gave me twenty dollars with which to replenish my wardrobe. I went to the store of the "King of Shirts," (Moody's,)[2] and stated to one of the clerks that I was a refugee from Texas, and had just received some money from General Hamilton, and requested him not to extort on me. Finding I was from Texas, he asked me if I knew any persons by the name of Swearingen. I told him I did; that I had a brother-in-law of that name;[3] that he came to New Orleans about a year and a half ago; and, after I described him, he told me he knew where he was, and that he would write to him. Having dispatched a note to him, giving him my address—"The Soldiers' Home," New Orleans—on the third day he was down to see me. He bought me a suit of clothes and gave me some money to meet my expenses while in the city.

I then had a brief narrative of my adventures published in the New Orleans *Times*.[4] Governor Wells[5] saw it, and as there were several refugees from the Calcasieu at New Orleans who knew me, and among them the notorious "Jayhawker," Dr. Dudly,[6] the governor was at no loss to find me out, expressing his great joy at my almost miraculous escape. He gave me a letter of introduction to General Banks. I was introduced to General Stone, chief of Banks' staff,[7] and after briefly telling him all that was necessary in such a case, he sent me to report to General Franklin, commander of the 19th army corps,[8] at Franklin on Bayou Teche.

I went to Franklin and reported to the general. As I was in the provost marshal's office one day, who should step in but Dr. Hubbard, the same who betrayed me to Major Blair. I knew him as soon as I cast my eyes on him, and he recognized me. I riveted my eyes on him, but he could not stand my scrutiny; he turned his face from me every time I looked at him. I wrote at the desk a brief note, addressed to the provost marshal, asking him who that officer was, telling him he was the doctor who, on the 16th of January last, betrayed me at New Iberia to the rebels; telling the provost marshal I did not now care to have any proceedings instituted against him, as I was now in safety, but I wished to expose his treachery. He belonged to the 165th N. Y. V., or 2d regiment, Duryea Zouaves.

When the army started for Alexandria, I was sent by General Franklin in the advance, with the first brigade of cavalry.[9] When we got to Cheneyville, within about thirty miles of Alexandria, we learned that General A. J. Smith, with the 16th army corps, had taken Fort De Russe,[10] on the Red river, and that Taylor's army passed out between Alexandria and Cheneyville three days before we got there. Had General Franklin known this, and the 19th army corps left Franklin three days sooner, so as to meet the gunboats and the 16th army corps at Alexandria, Taylor and his whole army would doubtless have been captured.

I was but a few days in Alexandria when I saw, coming in from the Calcasieu district, several of my old Union friends, and a good sprinkling of rebels, to take the oath of allegiance. The latter did not regard the oath as binding on their consciences, that is, if they ever possessed such an article; for, when Banks evacuated Alexandria they all went back to the rebels. Not the last nor least important among them was Louis Texada, who was the "life and blood of the conspiracy" in that section, and who afterwards accepted a commission as captain in the reserve corps of the Confederate army.[11] Those double-distilled traitors are now claiming the rights of citizenship, and voted at the election on the 6th of November, 1865, under the President's proclamation of the 8th of December, 1863.[12]

As Governor Wells was born and raised in Rapides parish, he knows them all; and by comparing the registry of the voters with their property estimate from the tax book of 1861, he can see at a glance those who were exempted by the President's proclamation of May 19, 1865,[13] as being worth over $20,000, and those who took the oath in April and May, 1864, and since aided and assisted "willfully" in the rebellion; and as his new-fangled friends whom he appointed to office in preference to his old Union friends, who stood by him when "Bloody Bob" and Captain Todd were hunting him in the swamps, as well as the other "Jayhawkers," voted against him and for Allen,[14] after they, in their public assemblies, promised to give him their "cordial support," will he now see justice meted out to them as their crimes deserve? I have my doubts but that there was at least one-third of those who voted in Rapides parish who never took the oath of allegiance; and I further doubt but that more than half the planters on the river and bayous are under the ban of the President's proclamation of May 19, 1865, on account of their being worth upwards of $20,000, and unpardoned by the President, for "willingly" aiding and assisting the rebellion. Come, Governor Wells, you must see to this, and face the music whether you will or no; for this "little book" will travel further, and be read by more than ever read your fine letters to President Johnson.

Having digressed from the narrative of my personal history, in order to explain some incidents connected with the time Banks was in Alexandria, I will now take up the thread of my discourse, and reserve for the last chapter the digressions which, if in their order of date, would be scattered through this narrative in rather a desultory manner.

It was not many days after I reached Alexandria that the news was brought in of the capture of the Second Louisiana (rebel) cavalry,[15] and of their being on the march to Alexandria. I had a great anxiety to see if my old friend, Major J. D. Blair, was among the prisoners captured. As the column was wheeled round the rear of the court house, I hurried to its head and asked one of the Federal officers if Major Blair was among the captives; and, upon being answered in the affirmative; he called out for Colonel Blair, he having been promoted to lieutenant colonel since I had the honor of his acquaintance.[16] The major, as I still called him, stepped to the front when called, the Federal officer remarking, "Colonel Blair, here is a gentleman who wishes to see you." I took hold of his hand; I intended to have revenge, and I had it; I said, "Major Blair, how do you do?" he bowed, and answered, "How do you do, sir?" "Major," said I, "don't you know me?" "No, sir," with another bow, "I do not." "What!" said I, "you do not know me!" "Upon my word I do not, sir." "Don't you know the old man, John O'Brien, whom you captured last January at New Iberia?" "Oh!" he replied, grasping my hand and shaking it very cordially; "how do you do, sir? how do you do, sir? I'm glad to see you." I answered, "I am well, and more than ordinarily glad to see you;" that my name was O'Brien then, but my name was Haynes now. At this his countenance fell, and assumed an ashy paleness, and I exclaimed, I own with some asperity in my tone and gestures, "Major Blair, do you not remember, when you captured me, how you had the bandages torn off my arm, as though I were a dog?" He answered, almost inaudibly, "Yes," and hung down his head,

> "For he felt humbled, and humiliation
> Is sometimes good for people in his station."

I never saw a man so cut up. His officers standing round him looked the picture of despair, as the Federal officers and soldiers hissed him in a rage for his barbarity. As soon as there was silence I spoke to him, pointing my finger at him, and said, "Major Blair, let this be a caution to you hereafter. Remember the fortunes of war. I was your prisoner then, you are my prisoner now; should you have the good fortune to get back to your people, and should you ever capture a prisoner, treat him kindly." He replied, more audibly, "Yes, sir; yes, sir." As I turned away the Federals set up a loud shout, officers and men, upon seeing the kind of revenge I had taken of him. Many of the Federals said to me, "kill him;" and some were officers high in rank. I replied, "No, I am revenged; Major Blair is a man of education and refinement; that I believed that when he committed the act of barbarity on me he was under the influence of liquor; that from the castigation I gave him, and the apparent shame manifested in his countenance, I hoped it would make him a wiser and a better man.["]

I now received from General Banks a commission to raise a company of cavalry, which was called the First regiment of Louisiana independent scouts, and A. K. Bevers was appointed my first lieutenant.[17] I recruited in Alexandria from the Union men, who came in from the west of Rapides parish and Calcasieu, about twenty men, and went home to get more recruits.[18] It was five months since I was first captured, and when I got home, those who hunted me down like a wolf took to the woods in their turn, expecting if I should capture them that I would treat them as they would, or as they did, treat me; but they were sadly mistaken, for they only judged me by the standard of their own wicked hearts. My lieutenant lived in Calcasieu parish, about thirty miles southwest of me. I sent him home to collect the conscripts, and named a certain day and place for them to meet me. When I got to the place of the rendezvous, which was a creek swamp, about eighty men had gathered before sundown. Next morning I made a short speech to them, and when I closed the few remarks I had to make, I proposed that all who wished to join the scouts would step three paces to the front. About sixty volunteered, and forming them in a semicircle I swore them into the United States army, to serve during military operations in Western Louisiana and Eastern Texas.

One third of them had no horses, for the rebels Ivey, Smart, and "Bloody Bob" had captured them; many were entirely bare-footed, and some had scarcely clothing to cover their nakedness. These men had been hunted for the last two years by the rebels, to make them go to the war, and many a man had been killed previous to the time I was first captured, and double as many since. They hunted them with bloodhounds, which were trained to run negroes in "secesh times." A man by the name of Shannon,[19] who was afterwards the orderly of my company, was hunted down by dogs belonging to Joseph Chambers[20] of Rapides parish, after a race of ten miles, when he took to a tree to save himself from being torn to pieces. I afterwards captured two of those dogs and carried one to New Orleans, having lost the other on the route.

Those who were on foot I sent directly to my house; and as most of them could make brogans, I told those who were barefooted to hasten to my house and make themselves shoes out of some leather I had procured, while with the mounted men I went in search of horses. Horses were very scarce, as the rebels captured most of the horses belonging to the Union men, and when Banks' army came to Alexandria the rebels ran their horses off; I mean those who did not take the oath of allegiance. So I had to borrow of the Union men who had a spare horse, and was to return them after I got the men to Alexandria. I was gone but ten days from the day I left Alexandria till I returned, when I had mustered into the United States service one hundred and eighteen men, rank and file.

On the north of Red river, Captains Corley, Hawthorne, and Willet,[21] were making up companies. Dudley, though he had his orders before he left New Orleans, and got about twenty recruits then, might, if he had a mind, have made up his company with the advantage of the start he had of me; but instead of recruiting, he went about the country robbing trunks, and doing all manner of mischief,[22] till finally General Grover[23] suspended him from his command and drove him out of the battalion. The Union men on the north of Red river were not as anxious to join as those on the south side; perhaps it was because they did not suffer as heavily the persecutions which we had suffered. To encourage them to enlist, Lieutenant Governor Wells made a speech to them at Pineville, opposite Alexandria, promising them $300 bounty each.[24] He also told me to tell the Union men that they should have $300 bounty each; but the governor did not fulfill his promise, though he might have easily accomplished it through the legislature assembled at New Orleans in 1864, the senate of which he presided over till March 4, 1865, when he became governor of Louisiana. Though the governor forgot the scouts, he did not forget himself nor his sons nor his sons-in-law, for he and they have all fat offices, though they never took up arms for the United States Government; though I and my two sons were in the service, and losing my wife and one of my children, and having lost everything I had in the world; though profusely prodigal in his executive appointments of his rebel enemies to office, he never thought of me, nor do I know of but one of the scouts to whom he gave an office, and that was not much of one.

When the army returned, after the repulse at Sabine Cross Roads,[25] we could not go out and see to our families and carry them supplies; nothing had been raised in the country in the line of breadstuffs during the past three years. We could not get permission to go outside the lines after we were mustered into the service. My wife started with her teams and got as far as Polk's bridge, on Bayou Boeuf, when she was stopped by the rebels and plundered of everything she had.[26]

The rebels took a fancy to Mrs. Nichols, whom I mentioned in the first chapter of this narrative. She claimed the baggage as her's; but in searching my trunks they found some papers with my name on them, and also my daguerreotype. Captain Stafford—the same who was with Major Blair when I was captured at New Iberia, and with whom I conversed when a prisoner at Vermillionville—took my daguerreotype and put it in his pocket, stating that with it he could identify me, and if he ever caught me he would kill me. Had he known I was old "John O'Brien," he would have had no need of my daguerreotype. I have been informed that he denies all this, and says that it was Bob Martin or Bill Ivey. Well, Mr. Stafford, you need not father any more on those villains; they have to carry a heavy load of their own wicked deeds to hell, without throwing your mite on their shoulders. Besides, my wife knew "Bloody Bob" and "Bloody Bob [Bill]" as well, or, perhaps, better than you do. She had many an opportunity of forming their acquaintance by their frequent visits to my house without an invitation. Besides, there are four living witnesses yet, who know them as well as my wife, and who state they heard your name called, and describe you much better—so as you could be identified—than my daguerreotype does me, which likeness was taken nine years ago; for the wear and tear of nine years have made a great alteration in my mien and form; so, if you should ever wish to identify me, you have only to brush up your memory a little, and see if you can recollect what sort of a species of humanity you had for four weeks in Vermillion jail, in January and February, 1864, in the person of "Old John O'Brien." Were I vindictive, I could have been revenged on you. I might, on more than one occasion, have burned your plantation on the Red river, especially when the army was on the retreat from Alexandria, and you would have been none the wiser as to who was the incendiary.

Chapter 7

"How beautiful in death
The warrior's corpse appears—
Embalmed by fond affection's breath,
And bath'd in woman's tears."

THE 12TH OF May, 1864, is a day memorable in the history of Alexandria. The fleet and land forces had marching orders, and before the fleet sailed the town was discovered on fire. The boats dropped down the river, about a mile from the town, to prevent any accidents happening from the burning town. I rode into town that evening, to see my family before we marched. The town was on fire, and nearly burned—all the front portion of it, lying on the river. No account could be given of who set it on fire.[1] It was a very calm day, the flames could not spread across a single street, so the burning must have been the work of several persons.

The scouts were stationed at Mrs. Flowers,' about seven miles south of Alexandria.[2] A Dutch Jew of the First Louisiana cavalry was appointed major over us. His name was Henry F. Williamson.[3] I mention his name here from the fact that he was as great a tyrant and scoundrel as ever had command of a troop of soldiers. His tyranny, and the fact of the scouts not being let out to get their families out of Bloody Bob's reach, so incensed them that, the night before we marched, twenty-two of my company deserted, and made their way back to the swamps.

As we passed Governor Moor's house, it and his sugar-houses were on fire.[4] We halted at Judge Gervis Baillio's,[5] on account of some firing on our rear. We stopped here about a half an hour. Mrs. Baillio came to me, apparently much alarmed, and said, "Captain Haynes, for God's sake place a guard around my house and quarters; they are going to burn us up!" I did so, and saved the house and premises, though I knew Judge Baillio had then three sons in the rebel army. I saw no justice or expediency in the destruction of private property, where it serves no practical good and is without any military necessity—though, a short time before, the rebels burned my house and premises.

We had no fighting till we got to Marksville. We heard cannonading at Mansura, a little village three miles south of Marksville.[6] The rebel scouts appeared on the rear, and the scouts were ordered to the "front," which honorable though dangerous post we kept till we got to Atchafalaya river. I lost two men; and one was missing. The scouts had the honor of saving one of General Mower's batteries the last day of the fight; for, as the rebels made a flank movement to the right, unperceived, in the swamp, the scouts simultaneously made a flank movement on the left, and outflanked the rebel flankers.[7] I had the rebel's [*sic*] movements related to me a few days ago by a young man who was in the fight. He was, he said, at the battles of Sabine Cross Roads and Mansfield;[8] and so far as he could judge—and he said he was in the hottest of the fights at the two latter places—the fight at Yellow bayou, on the last day, was the hottest of any he had been in. He said all his company but six men, were killed or captured; he made his escape. General A. J. Smith appeared everywhere; he appeared to possess the power of ubiquity.

A bridge of boats was now formed across the river, and all the troops of each arm of the service crossed over in safety. I had been unwell for several days, and the morning after we crossed the Atchafalaya river I was taken seriously ill with the typhoid malaria and diarrhea, and was put on board a transport and taken to the St. James hospital,[9] New Orleans. Rest and the scientific treatment of Dr. Lee,[10] who had charge of the ward in which I had been placed, soon restored me to health and vigor; and as the state of the mind has a tendency to either depress or enliven the body, my mind was relieved from a load of anxiety by a note from my brother-in-law, Mr. E. A. Swearingen, informing me that he was downstairs and wished to see me. I went down from my room, and was happy to be informed that my family was in the city, but the children were in indifferent health, from the diarrhea, which they, as well as mostly all the refugees, had taken at Alexandria.

During the last four weeks that the troops stayed at Alexandria it rained but one or two showers. The town being small, and no water fit to drink but cistern water, on account of the number of troops, citizens, and refugees, these reservoirs soon failed; and as the well water could not be drank at all, we had to use the water of the Red river, which, at best, is hardly fit for a brute, and now it had become almost putrid from the dead carcasses of mules and horses, and the offal of slaughtered cattle and other filth. A few days after hearing from my wife and little children, I received a note from one of my sons, informing me that they and my quartermaster sergeant, Brooks,[11] were at the barracks hospital, New Orleans. They were taken with the diarrhea at Alexandria, and sent to New Orleans on board a transport.

The situation of my family rendered it necessary that I should be with them, as they were in a strange place, and entirely dependent on the rations furnished to refugees for their support. Being unused to such fare, they would have suffered severely had it not been for the timely aid of Mr. Swearingen, my brother-in-law. I now, through the partial kindness of Surgeon Lee, obtained my discharge from the hospital, though, indeed, I was far from being in a fit condition to "report for duty." But I believed I should get along better with my family than to remain in the hospital under a mental pressure from the anxiety I felt for my boys, as well as my wife and small children, and especially as Surgeon Lee furnished me with medicine to take at home. I now went to the barracks hospital to see my boys, and I found four more of my company there sick. My sons and sergeant were convalescent, and in a few days I obtained their discharge also, through the same process of reasoning with the surgeon in charge.

The scouts crossed the Mississippi at the Stock Landing. Colonel

Keily of the Second Louisiana cavalry[12] sent for me, having previously seen Captain Corley and Hawthorne, to have us agree to be temporarily attached to his regiment. Colonel Keily said that he was informed that the War Department would not allow any organized detachments independent of the regular line of volunteers, &c. I went with him, Major Fontain,[13] Captains Corley and Hawthorne, and Lieutenant Bevers to see General Dwight, chief of staff.[14] Dwight told us the same thing, and remarked that the War Department had more men than they needed, &c. This he must have known to be a false statement, for it was not six months afterwards when there was a call for 300,000 more men. He said the scouts could not get pay nor clothing if they could not agree to be attached to some regiment, and in doing so they would not lose their organization nor character as scouts, to serve only for the section of country they enlisted for; which was during military operations in Western Louisiana and Eastern Texas. Under these statements, and believing them made by General Dwight in good faith, I agreed to the proposal, with the proviso that Major Williamson should be removed from command of the scouts.

As soon as I gave my assent, a special order was issued attaching the battalion to the Second Louisiana cavalry.[15] The scouts were ordered to Fassman's press,[16] and Major Williamson retained, contrary to my express agreement with General Dwight. I told Dwight of Major Williamson's saying, respecting the battle of Sabine Cross Roads, that he did "not care a damn who whipped—the North or the South;" and that I did not wish to serve under him. Williamson had a grudge against me for this, besides his natural disposition as a tyrant. When they had us fastened in their clutches, and in, as it were, a jail to the scouts, they wanted the officers to certify to the pay-roll of the scouts who were in the hospitals; that the said pay-roll was a true record from the company's books of——— company, of the Second Louisiana cavalry. This I refused to do, and so did Captain Corley and Hawthorne; nor could we do so without certifying to a falsehood. We jointly sent a note to General Dwight, in the regular way, of this fact, and next day we were placed under arrest; and ten days afterwards we received an honorable discharge as "being too old to learn the duties of officers."[17]

The scouts were now turned over to the Second Louisiana cavalry, and a pack of Dutch Jews, for the most part, appointed in our stead; but their triumph was but short-lived, for I had a letter dispatched to the Secretary of War, with a brief statement of our case, that we were willing to fulfill our contract with the Government; and instead of the officers being too old to learn the duties of officers, the oldest of them were but middle-aged men. In the fall following, an order was received from the War Department disbanding the scouts, and consolidating the Second Louisiana cavalry with the First Louisiana cavalry;[18] and so Col. Keily, Major Fontain, and Major Williamson were mustered out of service.

When Dick Taylor had regained control in the Red river district, he issued an order requiring the families of all the scouts and Union men to be sent inside the Federal lines, their property confiscated, and their houses burned.[19] Had Dick Taylor no other sins to account for, (God knows he had enough for one, yea, for a score of bad men to account for,) this alone would be enough to make—

> "Hell receive him, riveted in chains;
> Damned to the hottest focus of its flames."

The very time the scouts were in their greatest trouble, their families came; some to Natchez, Baton Rouge, and New Orleans. The refugee houses were chocked-full of these poor, sickly, emaciated wretches; women and children, half naked and barefooted, had to travel on foot, from two to four hundred miles, to obey the mandate of this hell-hound of iniquity. And so the hegira of these wretched creatures continued, until Governor Allen put a stop to the tiger's rage; for General Smith, cooperating with Governor Allen, issued an order to stop the expatriation and burning of the Union men's houses. But this did the scouts no good on the south side of Red river; for "Bloody Bob," Ivey, the Smarts, Dave Paul,[20] Jew Benjamin[21] and his "Christ-killers," from Alexandria, were on hand as soon as the Federals were out of the way; and they did the work of destruction with celerity and cheerfulness. Not a Union man that stayed at home, and was caught, but was "shot with bullets as thick as they could stick in him," as was the usual phrase of those villains when they intended to kill a man.[22] And, strange to tell, when the Federals came to Alexandria, after the surrender, not one of these wretches were arrested; nor would General Hawkins[23] have anything to do with them. They and their accomplices are at home, cursing the "damned Yankees" at their pleasure, and enjoying the fruits of their bloody deeds, while the returned refugees are literally starving.

CHAPTER 8

"O, beauteous peace!
Sweet union of a State! what else but thou
Gives safety, strength, and glory to a people!"

THE CONVENTION OF 1864[1] having completed its labors and brought forth the constitution, which had been harped upon by the "unterrified" and commented on with so much acrimony, a legislature had then to be formed, according to its provisions, to make laws to suit the exigencies of the times. So every parish which was under the Federal protection had to be represented if possible. Lieutenant Governor Wells was at the time acting as governor, and as I had not lost caste with him then, or perhaps rather, as he could find no person else who would venture within the vicinity of Colonel Harrison's[2] "man hunters," gave me the appointment of "sheriff of Madison parish." I knew Madison to be a rich parish, and thought I would realize out of the office enough to start me to housekeeping. But O, Moses! I never was so badly fooled in my life, for the sheriffalty proved an eggshell without meat; for when I got to Milliken's Bend I found, to my great mortification, the parish depleted of its inhabitants. Those who did not go into the rebel army, abandoned the parish, except here and there a two-faced, one-sided rebel, who was smart at stealing cotton and swearing to lies, to get supplies to furnish the guerrilla captains—Dishroom, Hedricks, and Lusk,[3] and their companies—from the treasury department at

Vicksburg. An occasional copperhead Yankee would crawl in, such as ex-Captain Deweese,[4] and some minor small fry, as E. D. Richardson and Charley Swan.[5] I verily believe these scoundrels would swear the legs off a pot, if they could get a pound of cotton each for them. Here I was with my family, and with nothing else but the little stock of provisions I drew at New Orleans from the post commissary; and as my family was sick and could not eat Government rations, I had to supply them from the market, which I did as long as the money which my wife got from her brother lasted; and two hundred dollars, which I received for a couple of yokes of steers, I loaned to a widow at Alexandria to bring her along.

I could not now be considered a refugee; I was "sheriff of Madison parish," and, therefore, could not draw rations, unless, as Colonel Young[6] said, I would go to Vicksburg to the refugee house or go North, and he would send me there. Having lived in the South twenty-eight years, my wife and children born in the South, and not having means to purchase clothing sufficient to protect us from the inclemency by day, nor bed clothing to keep us warm by night, in a Northern climate; my children sick, (I lost one in New Orleans,)[7] my oldest son an invalid on furlough, my own right arm broken, and broken so close to the shoulder joint that if I had been raised to manual labor, I was now unable to perform it. So here I was,

"Like patience on a monument smiling at grief."

Colonel Young recommended me to Col. Samuel Thomas, provost marshal general of freedmen for the district of Vicksburg,[8] to be appointed provost marshal of freedmen for Madison parish. I went to Vicksburg and showed the colonel my "papers," which were satisfactory enough. He gave me the appointment, but, like the sheriff's office, it proved equally as abortive. When I asked Colonel Thomas how I was to get supplies for my family, he said the commander of the post at Milliken's Bend would let me have rations. Colonel Bryant[9] told me he could not, that Colonel Thomas should have given me an order on one of his commissaries. I wrote this reply to Thomas; he informed me he had to "certify on honor" that the rations issued were for contrabands or officers, and as I "was not an officer then" he could not let me have rations. There was no stipend attached to the office, nor was I allowed to charge any fees for auditing the books and accounts, quarterly, between the lessees and the freedmen; so I was going to resign an office that would not furnish me with supplies, fees, nor stipend. How I was to live I did not know.

The lessees seeing that I was active in suppressing crimes and misdemeanors in their neighborhood, that I was very useful to them, much more so than the whole regiment of the 46th U. S. colored infantry,[10] offered me ten dollars a month each, to visit their plantations once a week and rectify the refractory negroes, and hunt up the mules and horses which the loose darkies were continually stealing. I now was busily employed, and indefatigable in my endeavors to maintain law and order in the settlement, and made several arrests of notorious rascals, who were killing cattle and stealing hogs and mules from the lessees, and sent them to Vicksburg to Captain Curtis, the provost marshal.[11] My proceedings were satisfactory enough with Captain Curtis, for in the case of every able-bodied man who was accused of a crime, the captain would tell him he would send him to the Alton penitentiary during the war, or gave him his choice to go in the army; and as Massachusetts had sent her delegates to the rebellious States to enlist men to fill her quota for the army, they were offering $350 bounty for every recruit they could get; and the captain, to "turn an honest penny," would sell the colored men thus obtained to those recruiting sergeants for $325 each. By such means as these the captain amassed a handsome fortune, and about the time he was relieved from office he had an agent offering $40,000 for a plantation. Should the captain see this "little book," and dispute the foregoing statement, I refer him to Mr. Morea, the detective.[12] And as he told this to the captain in the presence of General Dana,[13] I presume he would tell it over again to anybody who should think it worth their notice to ask him.

I saw directly that Colonel Thomas' views and mine with regard to the moral training of the freedmen in their new position did not correspond, and we did not have long to wait till an occasion occurred which exploded the mine and blew all my hopes of "biscuit, cakes, and butter into the middle of next week." It was this: there was a notorious scoundrel by the name of George Clark,[14] originally from Mississippi, staying upon the Parker plantation on Walnut bayou.[15] He was a terror to the negroes whom Parker left on the plantation. He was in the commission of every offence, large and small. He was a large and athletic man, as well as a daring villain, and as to scruples, he had none in committing any crime. He one night went to the house of Colonel Graves,[16] a citizen on Little Tensas bayou, and fired, as he thought, at Mr. Graves, but it happened to be one of his servants, and killed him. He killed and took off several hogs from an old lady, Mrs. Wells.[17] He and his accomplices killed three large hogs of Mr. Barker's,[18] which were in a pen about ten feet from his door, about thirty chickens, and killed four poor hogs in the yard, which were not fit for use. He went to the house of John Guider[19] in the daytime, in company with another negro by the name of Paul, and killed in Guider's lot, before his eyes, three hogs, one of which would weigh three hundred pounds. They were armed with muskets and pistols, and told the servant girl they were coming back after corn. Hearing of this case I went to Parham's plantation.[20] The negroes there saw them pass, and one, Jesse, bought half a shoat of them. Jesse seemed to be an honest fellow, and willing to go with me and identify them; I pursued them. When I got to Parker's I made inquiries if they knew anything of them, but none would confess to seeing the robbers. I went into a cabin and saw a piece of very fat fresh pork on the table, and asked the woman who lived there where she got that meat. She was loth to tell at first, knowing me to be the sheriff and provost marshal, and became alarmed. Upon my assuring her I only wanted to know how she came by the meat, and who gave it to her, she then told me it was George, and pointed to the house where he lived. I went into the room, and behind the door I found a large shoulder and the hog's head, and on the bed I found another shoulder and some pieces under a blanket. I also found a loaded gun. I now could find out everything about George Clark, and learned where his comrade lived, and his name. Paul lived at the Cooper plantation,[21] two miles further down the bayou. I went there, and the Parham negro saw and identified him. I then arrested him and gave him in charge of my aid, while I searched the house. I found no meat but a little in a pot; and upon further search I found a large bowie knife, bloody, and a gun; the knife I have got yet. I started to carry him to the Bend; his friends interceded for him, and laid all the blame on Clark. Paul told the whole story as near as a roguish man could tell. They agreed to pay me fifty dollars for Paul for his share of the damage. I did not then know how much damage they had done, and finally, on paying the money, I let him go. George having ran off when he saw me coming, and learning that I took the meat and gun, and also about thirteen bushels of corn, which I sold, and paid the money to Guider. George now went to Vicksburg and told Col. Thomas that he killed the hogs, but he said he had to have meat, and told of Paul paying me fifty dollars. Colonel Thomas fined him ten dollars and sent him home, telling him fifty dollars was enough to pay if he had killed a man; in a few days after, he came to my house demanding his meat, and corn, and gun, and told of the protection he had from Colonel Thomas. I wrote to Colonel Thomas what George had reported of his encouragement to him, and asked him if he could deny it. The colonel was silent as regarded all this, but before I was aware of my course offending the colonel, I was "reduced to the ranks," and was superseded in the provost marshal's office by a Lieutenant Cheney,[22] and orders issued to his assistants that if I meddled with leased plantations or freedmen, to have me arrested. This order was copied in his letter of revocation to me as assistant provost marshal of freedmen. I still kept arresting the thieves and sending them to Captain Curtis; and I had the temerity of displeasing Colonel Thomas, so far as to send copies of our correspondence to the State authorities, which made (I presume) the colonel to tell his deputies that I had a right to arrest all delinquents and bring them to trial. This same Clark went last spring, February 3, to Guider's and shot at him in his house, and if it had not been for a looking-glass which diverged the ball from its course, would have shot Guider in the head. I arrested him in Vicksburg for this crime also, and after being tried by a military commission, and all the facts of the case proven against him, together with his own confession, he was turned loose. I then affirmed I never would arrest another rogue; I saw no use in it.

About the first of December, 1864, the troops evacuated Milliken's Bend, and about Christmas my two boys came to me, being discharged when the scouts were disbanded.[23] I rented fifty acres of land, and was preparing to plant, when some of Colonel Harrison's "man hunters" paid me a visit; so my boys had to take to the swamp, and my friend Guider's wife, for whom I had been embroiling myself with Colonel Thomas and the negroes, told the Confederates that I and my sons were in the Union army, and they came to my house to capture me and my boys. We built a little cabin in a canebreak [*sic*], and kept concealed till the Mississippi overflowed its banks. The Confederates went back to the hills, and I went towards Vicksburg and engaged to the Planters' Association as lieutenant in the home guard scouts, and my sons as privates.[24] I was invited to stay at Young's Point by a mongrel Yankee lessee and general cotton thief, as I afterwards found him to be. He had a partner by the name of McCullough,[25] an Irishman from Vicksburg, a regular thief and harborer of thieves. These "noble pair of brothers" brought with them a lot of stolen horses and mules, which they bought from negroes in Mississippi. I found the owner of some of them, a man by the name of Watt.[26] Watt got an order from the provost, directed to me, to seize the horses and mules and deliver them to Watt, which I did. Watt compromised the case with Swan and McCullough; and though he offered me a liberal reward if I would get him the horses and mules, after his leaving my house to return three weeks following, I have not seen him since.

During the overflow of the Mississippi the guerrillas were cut off from any and all approach to Young's Point, by the crevasse in the levee there, and all approach to Vicksburg, except by water. We had nothing to do now, as the high water cut off all fears of the guerrillas, and we having no means of support, the prospect of living was gloomy indeed. In the overflowed land at Young's Point there grew a species of blackberry, called the dewberry, and as it was the forwardest fruit that ripens in this latitude, I concluded to gather some and take them to Vicksburg. They were obtained only by boating and wading. I sold the first lot for fifty cents a quart; and so on, in a reduction of prices, till they were all gone. By this means I obtained about seventy dollars' worth of provisions; but it was dearly purchased, for, through wading to pick the berries and boating to Vicksburg and back, my boys and myself took the typhoid malaria, from exposure and continually being in the water. The overflow was so great we could go nowhere without a boat.

When the river commenced falling I went to the plantation I had leased, and planted about seven acres of corn, some with a stick and some with a hoe. After peace was proclaimed on the west of the Mississippi the citizens began to return to their homes.[27] I went to tend my corn myself—my boys being sick. I was there informed by one of my sons that Swan and McCullough had gone to Vicksburg, and sworn before the provost marshal that I was an intruder on their Young's Point lease, &c.; and as I was from home, and could not answer to the summons, they procured a writ to have me ejected, and a guard also, to see it carried into execution. Having been informed of this, and my presence being needed with my family, I sold my saddle and my interest in the corn for $50, gave up a mule I had captured, and walked to Young's Point. The few articles of furniture I had were out of doors, and everything in confusion, and, worse than all, my wife sick. I resolved to trace my steps back to my old home on the Calcasieu river, Rapides parish. My wife was getting worse, and having no medical aid nearer than Vicksburg, I procured a team from Mr. McCallister,[28] a lessee, to remove me to De Soto landing, opposite Vicksburg, where I could obtain medical aid for her and my children, as I had now four of them on the sick list. The surgeon at De Soto, who had charge of the freedmen there, attended on my family. My wife grew worse every day, and as there was but one white woman at De Soto, I went to Vicksburg for a female physician. I told her I had no hopes of her recovery. She, too, upon examination, confirmed my worst fears, and by 7 o'clock next morning she breathed her last. I buried her on the levee, on the 27th day of July, 1865.

> "She died; but not alone. She held within
> A second principle of life, which might
> Have dawned a fair and sinless child—
> But closed its little being without light,
> And went down to the grave unborn, wherein
> Blossom and bough lay wither'd in one blight!
> In vain the dews of heaven descend above
> The bleeding flower and blasted fruit of love.
> Thus lived, thus died she. Never more on her
> Shall sorrow light or want. She was not made
> Through years or moons, the inner weight to bear
> Which colder hearts endure, till they are laid
> By age in earth."

And in her grave I buried my best and, almost, only friend.

Chapter 9

"I could stand upright
Against the tyranny of age and fortune;
But the sad weight of such ingratitude
Will crush me into earth."

I DETERMINED TO leave Vicksburg as quick as I could get transportation; and after selling a few articles of furniture—though at a great sacrifice—with which I did not wish to be encumbered, more especially as my oldest children, being very sick, were unable to do anything to assist me, and my own health was failing fast, from exposure, fatigue, anxiety, and grief. And, besides, I had but little money; and as I had to go to Alexandria by the way of New Orleans, I tried to hoard the little I had with the grasping avidity of a miser; so I went to General ———, commanding the post at Vicksburg.[1] He referred me to his adjutant, to whom I showed my discharge as an officer of the Federal army, and also my sons' discharges, and other "papers." This dignitary did not "see" that those papers would warrant him to give me "transportation," and referred me back to the general. This man "in brief authority" would not interfere with his adjutant's decision.

This ingratitude cut me to the heart, for this was "the most unkindly cut of all," which made me exclaim, with a bitterness already soured by misfortune, "How is this? You send rebel soldiers, who have been fighting against you for four years, to their homes, and you refuse me and my boys transportation who were fighting for you. This is a damned nice state of affairs!" I would have reported the case to General Slocum;[2] but seeing a boat coming down the river, rounding the point, I hastened to the wharfboat, where my children were, and got on the boat—the "Henry Von Phul"—and, from my pecuniary inability, I had to take a deck passage to New Orleans.

On the fourth of July last I had written two letters, one to Governor Wells and one to his son Montford, naval officer at New Orleans,[3] briefly informing them of my abject situation; and as he had removed me from the sheriffalty of Madison parish, by the appointment of a rebel in my place, I solicitously begged him to give me some employment; but I got no answer. I thought, when I should see him in person, he would do something for me, seeing how poverty, sickness, and death had made me their sport; but, like all my other visionary hopes, they vanished like a mist before the sun.

The governor was polite and hospitable, he was willing to do anything he could for me, but, poor man, he could "see" nothing he could do for me; but I could see, by the New Orleans papers, that not a week scarcely passed but there were lucrative appointments made by the "executive." He wished me well, I have no doubt; but his wishes had about the same effect on me as those of the Pharisee had on the poor beggar, "Be fed and be clothed; but he gave him nothing."

He introduced me to Brigadier General Sherman, provost marshal, department of the Gulf,[4] to beg General Sheridan[5] would give me a letter to the commanding officer at Alexandria, &c.,&c.; which General Sherman did, with much urbanity and kind feelings. When I saw the governor I was scarcely able to walk, though I did not give up finally till, quite worn down from watching, grief, anxiety, and disappointments, the malaria—having, in my present state of body and mind, full control of my system—attacked me with a hot, burning fever, which rendered me delirious.

The stringency of my pecuniary affairs compelled me to seek lodgings for myself and family upon the cheapest terms possible. The hotel where we boarded is well known to refugees at least, and its character for bad fare had not abated since the year anno Domini 1864. I had not been able to leave my room, and had to pay a good lady who boarded at the hotel, surnamed "Commercial," to wait on my little children, the two youngest being dangerously ill. After two weeks we mended a little, and with the first Government boat I sailed for Alexandria. I should not have left the port then had I known the state of affairs to be as they really were. Speaking of this to Governor Wells, he remarked, "You never saw a set of worse whipped men in your life;" referring to the secessionists. But I found by practical demonstration that the governor knew nothing of the state of political feeling in his native parish, Rapides, or if he did, he wofully [*sic*] misrepresented it to me.

When we landed at Alexandria I went to General Hawkins[6] and showed him my "papers." He ordered me a team, and sent a guard of three men with me. About twenty miles from Alexandria I met a Union man by the name of McNutt.[7] He told me there was danger in my going out on the Calcasieu to live; that he heard a man say that if Captain Haynes ever came back it would not be well for him. I had to pass by what was once my home; my home no longer, for the ravages of war had done its work there. I went to an old quadroon woman's house by the name of Perkins;[8] her two grandsons were in the scouts, and her son-in-law, Johnson,[9] was killed by Bill Ivey. I stopped here, not knowing what to do, for all seemed gloomy and dark around me. I nor any of my children were well. The old lady was glad to see me, and sorry to hear that my wife was dead, for, as the old lady said, she was her best friend while she lived near her.

Next day I was sick, and laid down on the bed on the gallery. After taking a nap the old lady told me that while I slept two men on horseback came to the fence and inquired of her if old Captain Haynes was staying at her house, and that if he was she had better get shut of him, for if she did not, she would suffer the same fate as he; that the Pauls, the Johnsons, the Selonches, the Dunhams,[10] and all the county in fact, were against him. I learned the same from others, and was advised not to stay out in that section of the country. Provisions could scarcely be had at any price, and I being out of means, and not having found anything of what I left, had to get my supplies from the post commissary at Alexandria. I moved my children to my quartermaster sergeant's, Brooks, and one of the boys getting so that he could travel, I sent him to Texas to see his grandmother and uncle and aunt, who lived there, as we had not heard from each other in nearly three years. As I had to go to Alexandria for rations for my family, I went to General Hawkins and told him how the situation was in the country; of the threats made against my life, and that I had to travel armed, and was afraid to return the road I came; that I had nothing to do in the country, and even if I had, I was sick and disabled. He therefore ordered the quartermaster to give me employment. The wages were small, it is true, but he was crowded with employees, and did the best he could.

While I was in Alexandria I met, for the first time since I left New Orleans, Captain Corley of the Louisiana scouts, and after a long talk I asked him to come and take a drink. As we walked out of the drinking shop we had to pass through a narrow passage about six feet wide; I saw in my front five or six men blocking up the passage. I did not know either of them; in fact I paid no attention to them, being busy conversing with Captain Corley, when one of them, a young man, struck me with his fist, observing: "You treated my family kindly, did you, you damned———." He struck at me several times, but I warded off his blows, having, in my younger days, learned "the manly art of self-defence." Seeing he was not likely to do much damage in this kind of attack, he sprung at me, being doubly enraged, and grasped me by the throat and tripped up my feet. The passage being very narrow I fell against the wall with my broken shoulder. He then stamped me with the heel of his boot. I was so weak from a long sickness that I did not possess the strength of a ten-year old boy, and if he had not been prevented by Mr. Bogan[11] of Alexandria, I believe he would have killed me. I wish it to be known that I know the gentlemen who encouraged him with their presence in the gallery.

So badly was I hurt that for upwards of two months I could not lie upon my right side; my broken arm being so badly injured that I cannot now, November 12, put on my clothes without pain. My friend, the captain, abandoned me in the strife, and I did not see him for four weeks afterwards.

I was intent upon instituting suits for damages against Smith and Vansaux for shooting me, against Captain Stafford for plundering my wife, and against Joseph Texada[12] for bodily injuries. I went to a lawyer named Barlow,[13] who passed for a Union man, as he left Alexandria with Banks' army for New Orleans, when I got acquainted with him. After briefly stating my case, he told me he could not attend to it, as he was going north and would not be back till after court, &c., and referred me to Captain White.[14] I noticed Barlow in town every day, and he was there during court. I saw directly how matters stood with him. The poor pusillanimous creature was afraid to undertake my case, lest he should lose caste with the rebels, whom he now longed to propitiate.

I then went to Captain White, and after briefly stating my case to him, he said he did not think it was any use to institute suits against them; that, in fact, he was certain I could not recover anything. I then remarked: "Has the moral sense of the country got to so low an ebb that a jury would perjure themselves to keep from doing justice to a Union man?" He answered, "It appears so;" and further remarked that he was himself a Confederate officer, and would not undertake the case under any consideration, "if," as he remarked, "I must tell you the truth." I thanked him for his candor, and I would this day trust him before I would that *"ipse dixit"* Union man, Barlow.

There are two vices which I detest above any, or perhaps the whole brood of the balance, and they are ingratitude and hypocrisy. What Captain White stated to me as his opinion, I found verified in fact, when I tried to prosecute Smith and Vansaux for shooting me, and Texada for an aggravated assault and battery. I had prepared a written statement, briefly though, to present to General G. M. Graham,[15] foreman of the grand jury, of the cases I wished to bring before that body—aye! it was a body, sure enough; but without a soul. I opened the door of the grand jury room, no officer being stationed there. I was told I could not come in. I said I wanted to see the foreman; I was answered in the affirmative. I waited some time, and looked in again; the same question and answer. I told two of the jury whom I saw go in, that I wanted to see General Graham. They said he would come out presently. The door opened, but no foreman, but Big Pete Eddleman[16] from Lana Cocoa, or rather Sandersville, one of "Bloody Bob's" bottle companions; as he passed me going down the steps, he said, "You damned old thief and robber, what has brought you here?" He made the same remark to two of the jury whom he met on the stairs. I left the place, for I had reasonable fears of being assassinated. I should here make further statements of facts relative to this affair, but as I have discussed them in my letters to General Graham, the reader is referred to them in their proper place in this "little book."

In a day or two following I wrote a note to Mikey Ryan,[17] the judge, stating the circumstance of the case in detail; but he never answered my letter, nor was there any notice taken of my cases whatsoever. Oh, judge! oh, jury! "*Par nobile fratrum*"—or, as Byron has it, "*Arcades ambo*"—is but a mild term to apply to a court and its adjuncts who were sworn to "present no man through malice, and leave no man unpresented through favor."

CHAPTER 10

"The worm of conscience still begnaw
thy soul!
Thy friends suspect for traitors while
thou liv'st,
And take deep traitors for thy dearest
friends.
No sleep close up that deadly eye of thine,
Unless it be while some tormenting dream
Affights thee with a hell of ugly devils!
Thou elvish, marked, abortive, rooting hog,
Who hast been framed in the nativity
The slave of nature and the son of hell!"

IN CONCLUDING THIS narrative I will make a few desultory remarks occasionally, and a digression or two, which may serve as a sauce to the insipid monotony of a dry narration.

I have not had the advantage of any assistance, either written or verbal, in enabling me to give a more diffuse and, perhaps, accurate delineation of the many dark and bloody deeds which have been committed on both sides during the "Reign of Terror" in the northwest section of Louisiana. To do this is the province of a historian. Should the full history of Western Louisiana be written, it would present a picture of horrors shocking to the sensitive feelings of humanity. The cold-blooded murders, to say nothing of thefts and robberies; the barbarity with which these acts of violence were committed; the innocency of the "Martyrs of Liberty," whose blood was shed to gratify the wolfish thirst for blood of those human vampires, cannot be paralleled—if in the number of victims sacrificed, not in remorseless cruelty, even in the massacres of La Vendee, during the "Reign of Terror" of the French revolution.

One of the first of "Bloody Bob's" murders was the killing of Oliver Sanders.[1] He lived about eight miles southeast of Manny Sabine parish. He was a poor man, and had a wife and eight children. The reader may judge of their age from the fact of Sanders being a conscript under the age of 35 years. Sanders said, that before he would go to fight for the rich man's negroes, and leave his family to suffer, while the rich man stayed at home—as he could do, according to the exemption in the conscript act—if he had to die fighting at all he would die fighting at home. "Bloody Bob," hearing of this, went to test the truth of his statement; but, coward as he is in his heart—for I never knew a bloodthirsty villain to be anything else—he took a company of his vampires with him. Sanders was at home; but before he could prepare to meet them with any hopes of success, they had made a charge on the house and surrounded it. Sanders jumped for his rifle, which lay on a rack over the door facing the road, and in his attempt to get hold of it he exposed his body to the full view of his enemies, who poured in a volley on him, with dreadful effect to poor Sanders. He staggered and fell—fell across a sick child on the bed, pierced with eight bullets—a lifeless corpse. Oh! would not humanity shudder at witnessing such a scene. How heart-rending to the poor widow and orphans, thus to be deprived of husband and father in such a cruel and remorseless manner. I saw the grave of Sanders as "Paddy Carey's" men had me a prisoner, on their way to Shrevesport, under a charge of high treason. It was on the side of the road, opposite Sanders' house, about fifty yards from the house. His wife and some neighboring women had to bury him, for the men were either in the army or in the woods.

To follow in detail the number of murders committed by this wretch, whose acts of barbarity would not entitle him to be classed with the human species, would fill a volume in octavo. I only select the case of Sanders as being among the first of his deeds of cruelty; and these cruelties were not only sanctioned, but applauded by the sensitive, the elite aristocracy of Western Louisiana.

"Bloody Bob" was, or is, or has been, a quadroon Indian, and inherited, in a most felicitous but unhappy manner, the inhuman thirst for blood of his dusky progenitors. It is strange, but it is a fact, that the mixed races, even to the fourth degree, exhibit, when provoked, all the malign propensities of the Indian family. There was not an instance of any of the mixed stock showing any mercy, even to their nearest relatives. For instance: Bass betrayed Connelly, his first cousin; Joe Strather shot his uncle, Alexander Strather[2]—the latter was a full-blood white, but his nephew was an Indian quadroon by the mother's side; Obi Johnson[3] killed his cousin. Josiah Johnson's sons, Charles and Budd,[4] were of the black stock, and so was Curly;[5] and as Calcoat[6] married the Johnsons' sisters, it would seem he became inoculated with their thirst for blood, for he was as ravenous as the others. There were also Jim Groves, a half-breed negro from Rawhide, and Carrol [*sic*] Jones, who was a slave born, and would vie with death and hell in all the propensities which constituted an incentive to the commission of vile atrocities.

But as an offset to this catalogue of the "colored stock," I will present the reader with a brief enumeration of the Caucasian family who figured in the bloody drama in Northwestern Louisiana. First and greatest among them were General Dick Taylor and General Morton [*sic*]; their "orders" can be produced, if necessary, to prove the wicked deeds which they had committed. Murder, arson, and plundering of the Union men was the order of the day. Next comes Bill Smart, Doctor Smart, Reese Smart, Bill Ivey, Dave Paul, Jake Gunter, Joe Chambers, Benjamin, Captain Lynn,[7] and a host of others; also, Doctor Dudley, Levi Boyd,

Wesley Lovin, Bryant Presly, Josiah Strather,[8] and Jerry Cloud.[9] The latter were Union men; but, so far as I knew or heard, none of them committed any murders except Dudley, who, I am told, killed a man at Hickory flat, for being the cause of several Union men being shot.

All the conscripts who were captured south and north of the Red river, were sent to Camp Pratt, in St. Martin's parish.[10] This camp was presided over by a "*genus homo*" from the Emerald Isle by the title and name of Lieut. Col. Ross E. Burk.[11] He was once a school teacher, and steamboat clerk, and now a merchant in Natchitoches; and from the accounts of the conscripts who deserted from this camp, this man was a second edition of Captain Wirz.[12] He has the unenviable reputation of being the inventor of the "*Devil's jacket.*" This was a flour-barrel with both ends knocked out, and holes bored near the chimes for the arms to be run through, the barrel resting on the shoulders, and in such a position that the unfortunate wearer of the garment could not reach his hands to the lower rim, to relieve him from the torture which four hours' wearing in the noon of the day occasioned; and when the offence was for uttering disloyal sentiments towards the Confederacy, the culprit had to walk before the guard house, bare-headed, four hours each day during his imprisonment.

The north side of Red river was also the scene of numerous atrocities; the chief perpetrator there was a Captain Smith, better known by the soubriquet of "Old Dog Smith."[13] This wretch, who was a counterpart to "Bloody Bob," was the terror of the Union men in Winn and Bienville parishes. He had a pack of bloodhounds to hunt conscripts with. A man by the name of Sandleford,[14] being one of his company, his wife sent him word she had nothing to eat for herself and children. Sandleford asked leave of "Dog Smith" to go home to provide something to eat for his family. "Dog Smith" would not let him go. Sandleford said he would go at all hazards rather than his family should suffer. "Dog Smith" told him if he did go he would pay for it. Sandleford went, but when he returned he paid for it, sure enough; for this hyena had him tied and shot to death at Mount Lebanon, Bienville parish, leaving a heart-broken widow and six children in abject poverty and distress. He also shot a man in Natchitoches parish, out of a tree, whom his dogs ran down, he leaving three orphan children without a mother. He also hunted down, in Bienville parish, a mere lad, with his dogs; the dogs ran him up a tree. "He was the only son of his mother, and she was a widow." This inhuman wretch fired his pistols at him without effect, and then ordered his men to shoot him, which order was obeyed by the cowardly wretches. The poor boy being mortally wounded, fell from the tree. The dogs being enraged by the shooting and hallooing of the human bipeds, and smelling the blood from his wounds, before he fairly touched the ground they covered him, literally tearing him to pieces before they could be taken off.

Reader, how would you feel to witness such scenes as these? and yet they were but the counterpart of almost daily occurrences. How did the poor, distracted, now childless widowed mother feel when the mangled corpse of her only child was brought to her door? Humanity shudders at its contemplation. Angels tremble at witnessing the fiendish deed, and devils shriek for shame at being outdone in diabolical wickedness by this human hell-hound. These atrocious deeds were committed in open day, in the face of heaven, and by the light of the sun; and yet, not a man of note or influence, either civil or military, would raise his voice to stop the bloody carnage. But, on the contrary, special orders were issued by Taylor, and others of his officers, to kill and destroy all who refused to obey their rebellious mandates. And strange to say, those men are now in favor with the Federal authorities, and not one of these "bloody murderers" have been brought to trial to answer for their evil deeds.

Dr. Lovick Pierce, father to Bishop Pierce of Columbus, Georgia, in a discussion with Shehane, the Universalist at Americus, Georgia, remarked that "he was glad there was a hell; and that God must be unjust if there were no place hereafter to punish the wicked who in this world committed such dark deeds of crime that would shame the powers of hell for their lack of will or power to equal them." And I, for one, am of his opinion. The laws of all civilized nations provide a punishment for every offence, according to its magnitude. And why not God, who is wiser than man, adopt the polity of which that of man is but a counterpart in a descending degree? Shall we receive a reward for our partial good deeds, and no punishment for our evil ones? If this be so, then I can say, "'Bloody Bob' and 'Old Dog Smith' fall to and kill the balance of the Union men." So far they have escaped with impunity. There is not a grand jury in northwestern Louisiana that will find a "true bill" against them for those crimes; and the Federal authorities will not interfere, knowing the state of affairs to be just as I have told them. But, on the contrary, those same men and their adherents swear that, so soon as the Federal army leaves the country, they intend to kill or run off all the returned refugees. Not only are these threats made as regards the returned refugees but I have heard many express it in private conversation; and I was informed by credible authority, when in Bienville parish, about the 1st of November, 1865, this blessed month and year of our Lord, that a gentleman made a speech in that parish at the court house, in which he stated that they intended to kill all the negroes who took up arms against their masters as soon as they were mustered out of service. And I here predict—and mark my words—that it will not be six months after the Federal garrisons are withdrawn from the Red river district, before they will have to be sent back again. And mark me, rebels of Louisiana, if the madness of your folly will drive you to such extremes as I have here noted, you will rue the day in which you were born.

CORRESPONDENCE

AFTER ARRIVING IN Rapides parish and finding the state of affairs totally contrary to that which was represented to me by Governor Wells, and finding the appointments he made of the civil officers in that parish and elsewhere to be, for the most part, that of noted rebels, and having conversed with many of the returned refugees and Louisiana scouts—officers and men—they expressing their disapprobation very pointedly at Governor Wells' course, I wrote the following anonymous letter to Governor Wells, addressed to him through the New Orleans *Times:*

Alexandria, La., September 18, 1865.

"I am the son of Marcus Cato, ho!
The foe to tyrants, and his country's friend."

To J. Madison Wells, Governor of Louisiana:

Sir: I would respectfully inform you, if you are not already aware of the fact, that your policy with regard to appointing notorious rebels to office has given great dissatisfaction to your old Union friends. Were such appointments but partial, they would have looked over it in silence; but it is the general cry all over the State. How is it—as in the case of appointing John R. Williams, sheriff of Rapides parish, a captain of cavalry in the rebel army,[1] and who, as you well know, fought against the United States Government till the close of the war, and from his wealth and influence most materially aided in the rebellion, and unpardoned by the President, he being worth over $20,000—how is it, I say, that you made such a man the chief officer of the parish? Was there no Union man in the parish you could trust with such an office? You did the same in Calcasieu parish, where the majority are still Union men.

Has the result of the elections of 1864 which made you governor so changed your nature? That you have done a great deal for the State no man can deny, and none is prouder of your success in your mission to Washington than your humble servant.

What astonishes your old friends the most, is the idea that by appointing your old enemies to office to reconcile them to you—"that the wolf may lie down with the lamb;" but you have not told us where the little child is that is to lead them.

The same hostility, bitter and bloody, exists against the Union returned refugees which drove them out of the country. The murderers, "Bloody Bob" Martin, Bill Ivey, the three Smarts, Chambers, Jew Benjamin, Dave Paul, and a host of other man-destroying villains, are at their respective homes, enjoying in peace the fruits of their bloody deeds. Your friends looked to you and hoped you would use your influence with the military authorities to have those bloody murderers arrested and tried by court martial. If you have done anything in the premises we have heard nothing of the result; and as to civil law being enforced against them, they claim that in their taking the amnesty oath the past is forgiven. Civil law, indeed! Why, you might as well go to law with the devil in the court of hell as to sue or prosecute a rebel in this section of the State!

It is a melancholy fact for those Union men to contemplate, who were your companions and defenders in your time of greatest need, how in your prosperity, when you could assist them in many ways, not one, scarcely, to whom you have given the least assistance. You have forgotten your promise of $300 bounty each to the Louisiana scouts, which promise you never did fulfill, though you knew very well the utter destitution to which they were reduced, especially when Dick Taylor expatriated their families, confiscated their property, and burned their dwellings, we have seen no effort on your part to redeem your promise to the scouts, though you might have easily effected it through your influence with the legislature, which sent Governor Hahn to the United States Senate,[2] and consequently made you governor of Louisiana. Not a dollar was appropriated, nor effort made by you to relieve the poor, unfortunate women and children, who had to travel from two to four hundred miles, half naked and barefooted, to be huddled into the refugee sink-holes at Natchez, Baton Rouge, and New Orleans, to die like rotten sheep through the sheer want of the proper necessities of life.

Believe me, Governor Wells, you have lost the confidence of your old companions, the "Jayhawkers," as our enemies call us. We little thought the plain old farmer would turn out a demagogue. Such an open desertion on your part of the loyal citizens of Louisiana, and your affiliating with your enemies, you will find a sufficient excuse for the few votes you will receive in the country parishes. For should a secessionist run for governor, you will find your newfangled friends, whom you have appointed to office, vote against you to a man, for they hate you now just as bad as they did when they hunted you and your sons[3] and the other "Jayhawkers" through the swamps in 1861 and 1863; for they may say, and perhaps with a great deal of truth, "that your appointing us to office"—

"Was for the sake of your dirty fee,
And not for any love for you or me."

I enter this "bill of complaint" against you more in sorrow than in anger, for had you remained "faithful to the end" none would have stood more faithful to you than MARCUS CATO.

Pineville, Rapides Parish, La.,
October 4, 1865.

"If you deny me, fie upon your law!
I stand for judgment. Answer! Shall I have it?"

Hon. Michael Ryan:

Sir: Permit me to inform you that on the 7th day of November, 1863, I was shot by one Vansaux and Archie Smith about eight miles from Hineston, which shot broke my arm, &c. On the 4th day of September, 1865, Joseph Texada committed on my person an aggravated assault and battery, in the town of Alexandria, in the presence of L. D. Corley, John Bogan, and others. I stepped to the grand jury room and desired to see the foreman, General Graham. John P. Eddlemond [*sic*] came out of the jury room, called me a damned old robber and scoundrel, and wanted to know what I was doing there. He repeated the same to two of the jurors whom he met on the stairs.

I returned home a refugee, about the middle of August last, and found my home was burned, and I found nothing of what I had left. My life was threatened if I stayed in the country (on the Calcasieu river near Hineston,) so I came to Pineville under the protection of the Federal garrison.

I am informed that the secessionists swear that as soon as the Yankees leave here, they intend to run off all the Union men out of the country. Knowing the threats made against my life, and being, when sick, beastly maltreated by a secessionist, cursed by a member of the grand jury whilst waiting to seek redress for my wrongs at the hands of the civil tribunal; not knowing, from the threats made against me, the abuse I already received, but I might be assassinated even at the door of what should be the temple of justice; so—

"I came awa' and left the session,
Seeing they were determined a' on my oppression."

If I have done anything wrong, I am here ready to answer for it. I defy the foul breath of calumny to lay anything to my charge and prove it. I can show a record from the highest authorities and challenge investigation.

If such proceedings are allowed to be carried on, vain is your assertion of the past being forgiven, of the "wolf laying down with the lamb." I shall hereafter want to see the beast's teeth extracted before I choose him for a bed fellow.

If you have power to put down these evil doings it is time you were at it—if you have, and will not, they will put you down.

Yours, very respectfully,
D. E. HAYNES,
Late Capt. U. S. Vols.

Alexandria, Louisiana,
October 10, 1865.

"Why hast thou chosen that cursed sin,
Hypocrisy, to set up in?

Because it is the thrivingest calling—
The only saint's bell that rings all in?"

Gen. G. Mason Graham:

Sir: As an humble citizen of this once happy country, now decimated of its inhabitants and rent asunder by the vandalism of friend and foe, I take the liberty of addressing you a few lines.

As you have consented to come before the public as a candidate for Congress,[4] I consider it a duty as well as a right to make such observations as I shall think pertinent to the position which you now occupy.

First, as regards some remarks which you made, as chairman of the unterrified Democracy, respecting the nomination of the parties brought before the public by that most august assembly. You launched forth into an elaborate encomium on the superlative supremacy of J. Madison Wells, the present governor of Louisiana. It is but a short time ago, and ye had a coil of rope bought to hang him with, and a shorter time still, ye hunted him and his sons and others, whom ye call Jayhawkers, in the swamps.

It is an undeniable fact, that if the great majority of those whom ye vilify as Jayhawkers were such, then all I have to say is that Governor Wells was king of the Jayhawkers.

You know, as well as any man in Rapides parish, that Governor Wells was at the head of raising the battalion of Louisiana scouts. He, Wells, made a speech to the scouts at Pineville, encouraging them to enlist, promising them three hundred dollars bounty, which promise, by-the-by, he never tried to fulfill, telling them that the country should be disenthralled from the ruthless grasp of a horde of traitors.

Then—another scintillation to illumine the panorama of Governor Wells' horoscope, which I may at some future time bring before the gaze of an admiring public—I have stated enough of the facts, which you know to be true, to damn him, as ye did damn him then, in the estimation of every secessionist in Louisiana, and more especially Rapides parish; or else you are doubly damned as a base sycophant for pandering to the sins of a man for whom you have had a mortal hatred for the last twenty years.

I tell you, general, you cut a sorry figure when you mentioned the twenty years hostility between you and Governor Wells; and how, contrary to all human nature, you gave him your "cordial support." Why, you are certainly a paragon of modesty! You must be more than human not to blush at the charity you manifested towards Governor Wells, for I declare, sinner as I am, I felt my ears tingle at the blush of modesty that overspread my physiognomy—for I really thought it was enough to make the devil blush, if he were possessed of blushing faculties.

There is another feature in the case, with which Governor Wells and you and others are concerned, which I will take the liberty of introducing to your notice. It is your loving sympathies for Governor Wells, and your hatred towards the returned refugees or Union men; you, as an individual, may deny any antipathy for the returned refugees. But let me ask you, as foreman of the grand jury, did you cause any investigation to be made with regard to the many cold-blooded murders committed on Union men in this parish? If you have, I have never heard of it; or if you have, your witnesses were those who participated in another "bloody picture in the book of time."

It is but a few days ago that a Union man was cursed and damned by a member of your grand inquest, right at the door of what should be "the temple of Justice," whilst seeking redress for his wrongs, he left, now knowing, from threats made against his life, the abuse he had previously received, but he might be assassinated. Though he informed Judge Ryan of these facts, and, also the clerk of court, yet he states he never heard of any action being had on the premises.

You cannot deny it, from yourself, that it would be futile for a Union man to seek redress for his wrongs in your courts. The general feeling among you being, as is strongly expressed by some, to run off all the Union men, or, as some express it, "kill 'em out at once, as soon as the damned Yankees leave here."

You know well that your taking the amnesty oath is considered among you as a forced-put affair, and that as a general thing you pay no more solemnity to its sanctity, than a dog would exhibit his solemnity at his father's burial. I know of many who swear they are ready to take up arms at any time and fight the "damned Yankees" over again, yea, for the next ten years to come. Some swear that a refugee should not work for them; others, that they would buy nothing from a refugee.

There is another item in the score of appointments made at that celebrated meeting of the "unterrified," and that is the nomination for Congress from the fourth congressional district, of General G. M. Graham of Rapides parish. I candidly confess that I do believe that you are the most eligible for office of any of the whole that were nominated that day. There is but one drawback, and unfortunately you cannot remedy the evil, for it has passed the eleventh hour of redemption: I mean the "*wee*" part you took in the rebellion, you being worth over $20,000 dollars [*sic*], unpardoned by the President, renders you totally unfit for such a position.

It is criminal in a man to deceive his friends knowingly; it is folly in a man to deceive himself; you had better look well to it, and see, before it is too late, that you are, if you get elected, deceiving yourself, your friends, and the whole people of Louisiana. For, according to the new test oath, every member of either House of Congress from the States lately in rebellion must swear that "they did not willingly aid or assist in the rebellion;" which oath you cannot swear to, nor are there three planters in Rapides parish who can take the test oath. Your opponent, Mr. Clayborn,[5] is still worse off, if possible, for he, in his address to the citizens of the fourth congressional district, tells plainly of his rebellious propensities.

Don't deceive yourself; there is not a man who goes to Congress but his antecedents will be as well known there as if written on his forehead; and the result will be, the South will find itself without a representation. The Republicans will make such laws for you as will suit themselves; perhaps confiscate your lands, pass a free negro suffrage law, and, as they have already threatened, turn loose in your midst 120,000 armed negroes.

Here is a point to test your modesty; inform your friends of your and their incompetency for their office; get some good Union man to run for the office who can take the test oath conscientiously, and as far as you can, whilst you have time, try to avert this dreadful calamity, which will be the inevitable result of the madness of your folly if you stubbornly persist in your present career.

ANONYMOUS.

Upon General Graham's receiving the foregoing letter, it was circulated broadcast over the parish that I, in connection with another gentleman, who knew no more about it than the "man in the moon," were the authors, and that I especially was disseminating the principles of the black republican party. I immediately acknowledged its paternity in the following letter to General Graham and his coadjutors of the grand jury:

Alexandria, La., Oct. 19, 1865.

I am not so deformed, for late I've stood
Upon the margin of the briny flood;
The winds were still, and if the glass be true,
With Daphnes I could vie, though judged by you.

The following are extracts of the letter of which the foregoing paragraph is a notice. It was addressed to Gen. G. Mason Graham, foreman of the grand jury of Rapides parish, and through him to his coadjutors of the jury.

As I have already published in this work my letter to Judge Ryan, which letter explains the main facts in the case stated in the forepart of this letter, I do not deem it necessary to reiterate it here.

Suffice it to say that the grand jury refused to hear me, and drove me from the jury room with much abuse and insult, and sent into the country for witnesses to prosecute me for robbery, for going with my command down the Red river, with the 2d Mass. Cavalry and 128th N. Y. Infantry, foraging for corn,[6] and also for going up Rapides bayou by orders from Gen. Grover, commanding post at Alexandria, to capture the robbers (Capt. Dennis & Co.,)[7] who were depredating on the citizens, the same who shot Tom Woodard,[8] and of whom Gen. Graham and the families of the other rebels who were in the rebel army stood in awe. I captured the whole gang, for doing which the whole settlement were much rejoiced, and none more so than Gen. Graham.

So highly did you appreciate my services, *then*, that you took me to your house and treated me, and the four men I kept as a guard, to a bottle or two of your choice *elderberry wine*, and you then asserted I done you a thousand dollars' worth of good. This was when you knew, and I mentioned the fact to you, you had not, nor would not take the oath of allegiance, and I mentioned the fact to you that you were suspected of disloyalty to the United States Government. Yet it made no difference with me in righting the wrongs I saw you were suffering under in your domestic affairs.

Yet, for all this, you have, in your official capacity as foreman of the grand jury, contrary to your oaths, neglected or refused to do me justice in having any wrongs righted; but, on the contrary, sent out for witnesses to try to find bills against me, for what I do not know, whilst acting under orders from the United States officers in command at Alexandria, and I then an officer of the United States volunteers.

You have, it appears, forgotten that I had any wrongs to redress, or any rights to maintain, how my house and premises were burned to the ground, without any military necessity, or by any orders from the Confederate authorities, how my wife's wagons were plundered, at Polk's bridge on Bayou Boeuf by the Confederates, whilst attempting to join me at Alexandria, though with tears, she begged for herself and her four small children, yet she was rudely and ruthlessly repulsed, and her property plundered, before her face, with as little remorse as if her captors were a band of Arabs, instead of the boasted chivalry of the South—the land of her birth and of my adoption. Yet I did not harbor malice against you or your people, but, on the contrary, when the army was on the retreat, when Gov. Moore's dwelling and sugar-houses were burning, I placed a guard around Judge Baillio's house and quarters, and prevented the burning of his premises, though he had three sons in the Confederate service then. In open honorable warfare I fought the confederates as a soldier in the United States army, and would again under similar circumstances, though I deprecate all useless devastations of property inconsistent with the rules of military discipline.

Setting aside my case altogether, let me call your

attention to the cold-blooded murders committed by Bob Martin, Bill Smart, Dave Paul, Bill Ivey, Benjamin and others, in this parish; the hanging, like dogs, of two superannuated men, Walley and Cloud, men who were as inoffensive as new-born babes; the killing of three men at Clear Creek on the ninth of May last;[9] the burning of houses unauthorized even by that merciless brute Dick Taylor; yet you have taken no cognizance of those open violations of law, though your oath bound you to leave no man unpresented through favor.

Have you ever examined into the cause of the massacres of the union men in the Calcasieu district? if not, let me jog your memory with some incidents which may afford some light on the subject. In the spring of 1861 there was an election held in this parish for delegates to the convention which caused Louisiana to cecede [*sic*] from the United States. Bill Smart and Louis Texada were candidates for the convention, and in the western portion of this parish they proclaimed themselves union men, but when they went to the convention they voted the State out of the Union.[10] The union men swore they would not fight against the United States Government.

The Confederate Congress passed a conscript act, and an exemption in that act of all persons owning twenty negroes, or five hundred head of cattle.[11]

The union men swore they would not leave their families to suffer, and go fight for your negroes, when you would not fight for them yourselves. You then sent out your conscript hunters to capture those whom some of your lousy aristocracy were pleased to call "Rosin-heels." There was no mercy shown them if found in the woods, whatever may be their business, they were hunted with bloodhounds, and many were cruelly murdered in their houses. When the yellow jacket battalion killed, near Hineston, two young men, Parker and Flyn, when the news came to Alexandria of their murder, Major Surget, Dick Taylor's adjutant,[12] was heard to exclaim: "Kill them, God damn 'em, kill 'em, that's the way to bring them in." The Louisiana Democrat, in an editorial of August, 1863, had black lines to be placed against the names of all persons who deserted from the Confederate army, or who took to the swamps, and, "when the Confederacy gained its independence, as sure as night followed day, there would be a dead reckoning made against them."[13]

Such were the counsels of some of the leaders of the Confederacy, in Rapides parish, men, who were too cowardly to fight, stood behind the scenes, encouraging rapine and murder, but as soon as Gen. Banks came to Alexandria, were first amongst the foremost to come and beg the privilege of kissing the "*Rail-Splitter's toe*" in the shape of the "Ironclad oath," thereby acknowledging themselves as "pardoned traitors."

When Banks whipped Dick Taylor on the Teche, the Texian soldiers broke for home, they robbed and plundered the union men as they traveled.[14] The yellow jacket battalion, whilst camped at Hineston, robbed the union men's houses of everything they could lay their hands on. Bedclothes, plow-gear, cow and horse bells, and even the women's shoes and little trinkets of jewelry. Bob Martin, and Bill Ivey's companies done the same and sometimes worse, for they took, even, the pieces of homespun which the women spun and wove with their own hands to cover the nakedness of their children.

Do you wonder there were recriminations committed for such atrocities? I know there were. I never justified them in doing so, but on the contrary advised against it.[15]

I appeal to Archie Smith, who was one of the two who shot me and broke my arm, on the public road near Smith's house, if I did not give protection papers to his wife, against any marauders who should come to interrupt her. I done the same for Mrs. Polk, and would, had Banks not evacuated Alexandria, have arrested, and sent to Ship island every scoundrel I could catch in the commission of any offence. I had procured an order from Gen. Grover to that effect.

"The evils which men do live after them,
The good is often buried with their bones."

So let it be with me. What I left was destroyed by my enemies, I carried nothing with me, I brought nothing back but sickness and sorrow, for the loss of my wife and child, who met a premature death from the hardships which they suffered from the persecution of their enemies.

I have been informed, that an anonymous letter, which you received a couple of weeks ago, was attributed to me and another gentleman in this parish, and it has been industriously circulated that I, as its author, advocated the doctrine of black republicanism. Now, sir, let me state to you candidly, that if the gentleman's name in question was left out, you might, as long as you please, and as much as you choose, (I use the pronoun you in the plural,) father that letter on me, and abuse me for being a black republican; it would have availed nothing with me. But as an innocent person's name has been dragged into notice, in connection with a character as black as you strive to make mine appear, I acknowledge the paternity of a certain anonymous letter which I addressed to you, and dated Alexandria, Oct. 10, 1865. I challenge you to point out one single sentence, or phrase, in that letter that can be tortured into favoring black republicanism; and as a proof of this fact, if you will send me the letter I will have it published, or otherwise I shall publish it from a rough copy in my possession. I gave you, in that letter, good wholesome advice which it would be well for you, and the country at large, to have taken in time. I gave you similar good advice five years ago, which you rejected with scorn, and which since you have wished in your heart you had taken. It was the giving of this advice, which rendered me obnoxious with you and your friends; that caused my arrest, and being sent under a charge of high treason to Gen. Kirby Smith—from whence emanated all my misfortunes, which caused me to "eat the bread of affliction and drink the waters of tribulation." I give you similar good advice now, which I am certain you will not follow any more than you've done five years ago; and I see the fruits of my kindness to you now, is being exhibited by industriously circulating my favoring black republicanism.

From the tenor of the prejudices circulated against me, I should stand a poor showing for my life, if twelve months ago, I should have the temerity of being audacious enough to counsel so august a personage as Gen. G. Mason Graham. It appears that the principle adopted now in Rapides parish, is that when you cannot destroy with your sting you disfigure with your slime.

> *"For, the little dogs and all, Tray, Blanch and Sweetheart,*
> *See, they all bark at me."*

I am a southern man in the true honest sense of the word, I have fought in the Florida war,[16] and, as a soldier who won some fame for his prowess in Nicaragua, I fought for you there too. But because I would support the Constitution of the United States, for the maintenance of which I took a solemn oath before you would admit me to the rights of citizenship, and because I would not willingly violate that oath by joining the rebellion, you consign my name and character to the blackest pit of infamy and scorn.

As you and your party were, for the sake of political favors, mendacious enough to endorse Governor Wells and all his official acts, giving him your cordial support, now let me show you what Governor Wells thinks of me, as well as some more persons equally as patriotic as he:

New Orleans, March 3, 1864.

Col. B. F. Flanders:

Dear Sir: The bearer of this, Mr. Haynes, is a refugee from Texas, and has suffered much. He wishes employment and I think deserves it.

If you can do anything for him, you will oblige me.

Yours, truly,
(Signed,) A. J. HAMILTON.

New Orleans, July 21, 1864.

Gov. M. Hahn:

Allow me to introduce you to Captain Haynes, a citizen of my native parish, a refugee, and a loyal citizen to the United States. Captain Haynes is trustworthy and fully reliable, and any attention will be thankfully acknowledged.

With regard, your obedient
servant,
(Signed,) J. MADISON WELLS.

Headquarters Military Division of the Gulf,
Office Provost Marshal General,
New Orleans, La., August 7, 1865.

By direction of the major general commanding this military division, I hereby recommend to the notice of the military authorities of Louisiana Captain D. E. Haynes, who has been active in the service of the United States; calling attention to the endorsement of his excellency J. Madison Wells, Governor of Louisiana.

F. SHERMAN,
Provost Marshal General.

The foregoing certificates speak for themselves. You cannot, without stultifying yourself, endorse Governor Wells, and slander me at the same time. You must either renew your twenty years' hostility to the governor, or else confess yourself a base and malignant slanderer. There is not a dog that barks at me and endorses Governor Wells, but his endorsement of me up to the 7th of August, 1865, is like a muzzle of adamant on the mouth of the slanderer. You can take either horn of the dilemma, and whichever horn you take it will gore you to the death.

As to your malicious presentment of me, if you were as foolish as you are malicious to find bills against me, you will see by the foregoing recommendation of General Sheridan how far your folly would carry you in presenting me, an officer in the United States army, and you a pack, for the most part, of unpardoned traitors.

Yours, with all the respect due
to you.
D. E. HAYNES.

"Ah me, what troubles do await
The man who meddles with the State."

Alexandria, La., October 28, 1865.

To His Excellency J. Madison Wells:

Dear Sir: I take the liberty of informing you of the state of public feeling here with regard to the coming election for governor. You may have seen ere this reaches you, how your quandam [*sic*] friends, whom you appointed to fat offices, are vacillating, nay performing complete political summersets [*sic*]; those who endorsed your policy in their public meetings, promising to give you their "cordial support," are now arraying themselves in solid phalanx to oppose your election, and giving to the ex-rebel Gov. Allen their more than "cordial support." The following I clipped from the *Alexandria Democrat* of October 25, 1865.

Communicated.

"*To John Kelso, E. North Cullom, M. Ryan, Henry Boyce, J. T. Hatch, E. T. Lewis, T. B. Waters, and J. J. Myers:*

The friends of Allen in Rapides are determined that they will not bestow their votes on any candidates for the legislature who are opposed to his election, and who would embarrass his administration. You are, therefore, respectfully requested to make known through the public press your opinions on the subject before the election.

A refusal on your part to do so will be construed as a declaration against him, and will be so proclaimed to the people.

(Signed,) Many Voters.

You might have foreseen this a long time ago, that your appointing your enemies to office would be no inducement for them to "cleave unto you" the moment they saw a chance to oppose you with any hope of success presenting itself by the announcement of a popular rebel leader; and such a one they have hit upon in the person of ex-Gov. Allen. The friends who would have stood to you "through evil as well as good" report you have alienated them from you, by your neglect or disrespect for them in not appointing them to office, when in nine cases out of ten you appointed to office, according to your own phraseology, "brigands, outlaws, and traitors, who have gone without the lash of the law too long," and not the least amongst them, you got into office the notorious conscript-hunter Capt. Todd, as a land office agent at Opelousas. You know better than I do how Todd flourished in your neighborhood in 1862 and 1863, and up to Banks' late advent in Alexandria, up to March, 1864, when his company dispersed; and when he thought the Confederate cause at a low ebb, like more of the double-distilled traitors, who were leading in the van of secession, as soon as Banks came to Alexandria were first amongst the foremost to beg the privilege of kissing the *Rail-Splitter's toe.*[17]

I have seen many of our old union friends since I have been here: Dr. Farquaher, John Strather, E. E. Brooks, Clifton, Cain, Wetherford, Milam,[18] and many others from the Calcasieu district; also the Chevaliers,[19] Boyce, Capts. Willet, Corley, and Hawthorne, north of the Red river, and others, not one of whom approve your course of treatment to the Union men, to say nothing of myself, though not one among them was more indefatigable or suffered more in the cause of the Union, yet you turned me out of office without assigning a cause, when the office became profitable, and appointed a pack of rebels to office in that parish.

When I was in New Orleans, you saw my utter destitution; poverty, sickness, and death, having made me their sport. You were so poor in your gifts of appointments that you could not find a hole or corner to stow me away in, though I could see in mostly every day's paper notice of the many lucrative appointments made by the executive.

When you were in Alexandria I tried to catch your eye to get to speak to you, but so intent were you in courting the favor of the lousy aristocracy, that I failed to *see* you. I do not know how it is, but "straws show which way the wind blows." I am not conscious of ever saying or doing anything to give offence to you, or any member of your family, up to the time you were in Alexandria, yet strange to say that your son Levi grossly insulted me, (privately though.)

You may, it is true, think, and so may he, that I have no influence here, and that it would be popular now to insult or assault "that damned old Captain of Jayhawkers," but let me tell you governor, sincerely, and time will demonstrate it, that I am more capable of doing a friend a service or an enemy an evil than perhaps you ever dreamt of. It is your interest, as well as your son's, to make as many true friends as you can, and as few enemies; for according to a card, published by your brother, Montfort Wells, in the Alexandria Democrat of Oct. 25, 1865, he gives you a character for paying your debts which is not at all to be envied.[20]

Don't think, governor, that I can rejoice at any evil report set afloat against you because I speak to you plainly both what I hear and know. "I am a plain blunt man that loves his friends," but will not flatter their follies nor hide their faults, especially when they grow as high as Mount Olympus."

Yours, respectfully,
D. E. HAYNES.

THE RECONSTRUCTION OF STATES.

By Captain D. E. Haynes, of Louisiana.
Washington, D. C., December 30, 1865.

To his Excellency Andrew Johnson, President United States:

Sir: In your message to the United States Senate of the 18th instant, you say that "the States lately in rebellion are yielding obedience to the laws and Government of the United States with more willingness and greater promptitude than, under the circumstances, could reasonably have been anticipated."

Having lately arrived in Washington, and coming from the interior of Louisiana, and being a resident of the South for twenty-four years previous to the rebellion, and living in the heart of rebeldom during the war, I may presume to say, without flattering myself, that I know something of the present political status of those people, of whom you are informed "are yielding a willing obedience to the laws and Government of the United States."

In August last, I returned to what was once my home, in Rapides parish, Louisiana, but found my home and premises in ashes, and divested of everything I possessed—having lost my wife and one of my children, through the hardships which they had to encounter, from the ill-treatment of our enemies. Every Union man who joined the Louisiana scouts, or who abandoned the country when the Federal army retreated from the Red river, was to be shot if taken. As an evidence of this fact the rebels shot one of my men whom they captured near my house. Rebel General Dick Taylor issued an order to burn the scouts' and refugees' houses, confiscate their property, and expatriate their families. This brutal order was but too faithfully executed. Thousands of women and children, barefooted and half naked, had to travel from two to four hundred miles; and huddled into the refugee sink-holes in Natchez, Baton Rouge, and New Orleans, where many of them died from the sheer want of the proper necessaries of life. Those who remained in the country were hunted with blood-hounds, and, when captured, butchered in the most barbarous manner. During the last two years of the war upwards of one hundred Union men were murdered in the Calcasieu district of Louisiana, west of Alexandria; even as late as the 9th of May, 1865, three Union men were murdered within sixteen miles of Alexandria.

After the cessation of hostilities many of the scouts and refugees returned to their homes, or rather to what were once their homes. They were first received with scowls, and after a little, as your Excellency showed clemency in pardoning the most notorious of those traitors, they became bolder, and publicly declared that as soon as the Federal army, or, as they expressed it, "the damned Yankees," are withdrawn, they intend to run off all the Union men, and more especially the scouts who took up arms against them.

On my way from Alexandria to where I once lived, a Union man told me that a rebel told him, that "if old Captain Haynes ever returned, it would not be well for him." The morning after my arrival in the vicinity of my old home, two men came to the house in which I was staying, and inquired of the mistress of the house if "old Captain Haynes was staying with her." She replied, "He was; and that he came to her house sick, both himself and his children." They told her, if she harbored him, she would share the same fate with him; and that all the neighbors—mentioning several of the noted rebels—were opposed to him.

I was informed by many of my friends that it was not safe for them to stir abroad, except in squads and well armed; and that, as for myself, I stood in imminent danger of being assassinated at any moment.

About the first of September last, I went to Alexandria, Louisiana, to try to employ counsel to sue for damages two rebels who shot me and broke my arm—they being noways connected with any of the rebel military organization of the so-called Confederacy—I could not obtain the services of any lawyer—no Union man there having the nerve to take a case against the rebels. I applied to an ex-captain of the rebel army—James White, of Alexandria. He informed me it would be no use for me to sue a rebel; that he was confident no Union man could get a verdict for damages; that he himself was a rebel officer; that he would not take the case upon any terms. I then remarked, "Has the moral turpitude of the secessionists got to so low an ebb, that they would perjure themselves rather than do justice to a Union man?" He replied, "It appears so, if I must tell you the truth."

On the fourth of September last, I was beaten violently by a rebel in the town of Alexandria. I was then convalescent from an attack of the typhoid malaria, and would, I have no doubt, been murdered but for the interference of a friend. I crossed the Red river at Pineville, opposite Alexandria, and took refuge under the protection of the Federal garrison.

At a called session of the district court at Alexandria, on the first of October last, I went to the grand jury room, and sent word to General G. Mason Graham, foreman of the grand jury, and candidate for Congress for the fourth congressional district of Louisiana, that I wished to present some cases before that body. After waiting a reasonable time I received no answer, and upon a repetition of my request, the door opened and out came a violent secessionist and cursed and damned and otherwise abused me, and asked me what in hell brought me there? I left the place, not knowing, from the threats made against my life, the abuse I had already received, and the conduct of this juror, but I might be assassinated.

About the fifth of November, I went eighty miles northwest of Alexandria. I was informed that a secessionist made a speech at the court house of Bienville parish, in which he stated the policy of the Southerners was to kill all the negroes [*sic*] who took up arms against their masters as soon as they were mustered out of the United States army, as well as to run off all the Union men.

I have heard similar expressions made use of as regards the killing of the negro [*sic*] soldiers, and it is a matter of policy for a Union man to make no comment upon the defunct Confederacy. I was told a few days before I left Alexandria, by a man by the name of John Stepney,[1] that he paid $20 for his passage from Alexandria to New Orleans on board the steamer Navigator, and when on board, before sailing, he remarked, in a conversation on the boat, "that the Confederacy was played out." He was threatened to be assassinated if he traveled on the boat, so he left the boat, and forfeited his passage money, before he would risk his life in the company with which she was freighted.

About the first of December, I was informed that Mr. Fitzgerald, the postmaster at Natchitoches,[2] was ordered out of the country for being a Union man.

In the fourth paragraph of your message, you say: "The people throughout the entire South evince a laudable desire to renew their allegiance to the Government and a cheerful return to peaceful pursuits." Methinks that the foregoing narration of what I know to be facts, and what can be proven to be such, in a portion of the South, exhibits anything but a "laudable desire for peaceful pursuits."

Your Excellency tells the Senate, and the nation in general, that you have an abiding faith that the actions of the rebels will conform to their professions, and your language applied to the entire South. Now, sir, if your Excellency will take the trouble to make an impartial investigation of the actions of the people of Louisiana as a part of the entire South, as regards the election on the first Monday in November last, you will find that their actions do not conform to their professions; but, on the contrary, are antagonistic to the laws and Government of the United States, and to your proclamation of May 29, 1865.

According to the constitution of Louisiana, no man is entitled to vote who has not been a resident of the State twelve months previous to the day of election, and three months in the parish. Yet in the city of New Orleans upwards of three thousand votes were polled for the rebel candidates by the returned rebel soldiers and registered enemies, who were absent from the State three years previous to the election. Thousands voted in the country parishes who never took the oath of allegiance, and many, very many voted, who were worth upwards of $20,000, unpardoned by the President.

The result of this election proved conclusively "their laudable desire to renew their allegiance" by electing to both branches of their legislature none but avowed rebels, with but one single exception.

This course of procedure on their part was encouraged and fostered by the backsliding of Governor Wells, who appointed to office, in the Red river country and northeast Louisiana, notorious rebels, whom he knew to be such, thereby giving the political control of the State into the hands of the enemies of the United States Government.

Subsidiary to the civil policy inaugurated by Governor Wells was his appointing militia officers all over the State, who, to him, were well known as leaders in the rebel army, though there were many whom he knew to be good and true Union men in the State, and among them the Louisiana scouts, yet he was studious to avoid taking notice of them either in the military as well as the civil policy of the State.

When some of the friends of ex-rebel Governor Allen put his name before the people of Louisiana as a candidate for governor, the rebels declared it would not do to vote for Allen then, though he was their choice; that if he were elected, the President may not pardon him; that Wells was known to be a Union man, and had great influence at Washington, and by voting for Wells, they would show their loyalty and obtain admission for the State into the Union.

As regards "the change in the relations between the two races," I do not think that the change has thus far profited either; and if the bill which has been brought before the State senate, on the fifth instant, be an index to the negroe's [*sic*] future fate, should said bill be carried into effect, (and it is more than likely it will, if no intervening power resists its effects,) would be by far worse than when in a state of slavery.

If the "reliable authority" from whom your Excellency derived your information would stroll into the interior of "the States lately in rebellion," lay by their insignia of office and travel *incog.*, instead of being toasted and feasted at crack hotels by rebel officers and civic traitors, whose aim is to mislead the Government at Washington, make their inquiries of the true friends of the Government, your Excellency would receive such information as would induce you to change the tone of your message of the eighteenth instant to the United States Senate; that Senator Sumner would have no cause to charge your message with "whitewashing the States lately in rebellion."

It is a melancholy fact, as well as a reliable truth, for the Union men of the South to contemplate that, after having stood the brunt of persecution and untold of hardships during the "reign of terror," in the heart of the enemy's country, that now when the blessings of peace dawned upon the country, they find themselves persecuted by their enemies and abandoned by their friends—they finding no redress for their grievances in the civil courts of the States, nor can they find employment from the Federal officers in the civil departments; but, on the contrary, rebels from the rebel army are employed in preference to Union men. Let me state to your Excellency a case in point.

About the eighteenth of November last I arrived in New Orleans, for the third time a refugee, disabled from my wounds, and destitute of every or any means to educate or support my five motherless children. A discharged officer from the United States volunteers, I made application to Judge Kellogg, collector of customs at New Orleans.[3] My application was recommended by the Hon. John Hawkins, Hon. R. King Cutler, United States Senator, and Hon. B. F. Flanders, special agent of the Treasury Department, New Orleans.[4] Five days after my application, Judge Kellogg made some fifteen or twenty appointments, more than half of whom were rebel soldiers. These facts can be proven, if necessary; yet, for three weeks I remained in New Orleans, I had no hearing from Judge Kellogg.

Should the present political status in Louisiana continue in the same progressive ratio during the ensuing six months as it has in the past, the Union men will have to abandon the State, or fall victims to the bloody policy that drenched them in their blood during the last three years of the war.

I hope the Executive arm at Washington will not be so hampered, from the information derived "from reliable sources," as to leave the returned refugees of Western Louisiana to their fate, through an overweening, though well-intended, desire for a hasty reconstruction. I hope your Excellency will be dictated by that noble principle of patriotism and Christian charity which has ennobled your past career as well as your present administration. As to Governor Wells, if continued in office, he may as well send a cargo of coffins to the Red river district of Louisiana—his old home—that when "Bloody Bob" Martin and old "Dog Smith" shall once more begin their work of death, the martyred refugees may receive the semblance, at least, of a Christian burial, and not be buried like dogs, as they have been under the reign of terror during the rebellion.

With the highest esteem for your patriotism and love for the Union, I subscribe myself your Excellency's obedient servant,

D. E. HAYNES.

EMIGRATION TO THE SOUTHERN STATES.

Washington, D. C., January 24, 1866.
Col. Chase A. Stephens,
General Stock Agent of the United States Mutual Protection Company:

Sir: In accordance with your request, I will briefly give you my views as regards the efficiency, with respect to the amount of good the company may effect in encouraging settlements in the Southern States; and the probable results to settlers emanating from a cheerful compliance and ready co-operation of those who are in want of good homes and homesteads, with the terms which the company holds out to emigrants.

The gold regions of California never offered more tangible inducements to the adventurer than the cotton regions of the South now offer to the agriculturist. The Southern planter, divested of the slave monopoly, finds himself in possession of vast open, but uncultivated, estates, which from the new order inaugurated by the suppression of the rebellion leaves those vast fields of enterprise, which were cleared and brought into a high state of cultivation by the sweat and blood of the slave, open to the emigrant, which by industrious perseverance would be sure to yield a very liberal reward for his labor.

Having been a resident, and of the Southern (cotton) States for twenty-four years previous to the rebellion, and living in the heart of rebeldom during the war, I cannot be accused of flattering myself when I state, that I think I know as much of the real value of this section of the United States, to emigrants, as, perhaps, one to the manner born; and, not being a stockholder of the Mutual Protection Company, it is not my fault, but my misfortune, that I am not; nor have I any lands to rent or sell to emigrants, which might be thought to induce me to give encouragement to emigration, in order to sell or rent lands or make a profitable investment in the stock of the company; I therefore, sir, give you my honest views practically drawn from long experience and practical results.

First, as regards the emigration to the South of loyal Union men, and settling in small colonies of from twenty-five to one hundred families, within a reasonable distance of each other, say from five to twenty miles distant, so as to form a religious and political nucleus round which the loyal Union men of the South would rally, for protection or support in case of an outbreak amongst the disaffected.

Whatever may be the disaffection to Northern Union men at this present time, it is not half so much so as the hatred to the Southern Union men, whilst an influx of emigration of loyal Northern men, under the protection of the United States Government, would so neutralize any outpouring of the spirit of hatred which is now manifesting itself in the breasts of the disaffected, from the results emanating from well-cultivated plantations, mutual intercourse, and above all and most important to the Southerner, a sure and effectual protection of life and property, which is one of the great sources of annoyance to a true Southerner regarding the present status of the negro; nor will this fear be allayed by the action of the present Congress with regard to the right of suffrage to the colored people of the District of Columbia, but, on the contrary, will so increase their alarm, lest the reconstruction policy of Congress in not admitting the States lately in rebellion keep them in "*status quo*" till they are willing to embody in their constitutions the right of suffrage to the negroes.

Under this hypothesis, and I think I state the true pulsation of the southern heart—seeing their armies crushed in the rebellion, their schemes of reconstruction baffled, and to them the hateful and cursed policy of negro suffrage looming high in the dark horizon of their political zenith—they will stretch out the right hand of fellowship to the Northern emigrant, and grasp with avidity the hand of hope and the arm of strength which he sees ready to launch his fortunes in the same bottom with himself. This army of emigrants would prove more effectual in maintaining peace and order in the Southern States than a standing army of 100,000 men. Not only would its physical force in point of numbers be felt, but its moral force would be tenfold more conducive in the mutual benefit arising to both parties in the cultivation of the soil, in their social relations, and in the all-absorbing fear of insurrection from the colored population. Whether the Southerner has really any true ground to dread an outbreak of this nature or not, is not the question. This story has been rung in their ears, from their cradle to their manhood, till it has become a part of their creed to believe that when the negro becomes a free agent, nothing but bloody murders and insurrections are the concomitant results of his freedom.

With regard to the prolific production of the soil, it varies according to the nature and locality. That which borders on the rivers and bayous being the most prolific; the Mississippi swamp lands, the Red river, the Atchafalaya river, the Washita [*sic*], and others of minor note, being considered the best lands in the State for cotton, especially that which lies north of the parallel of latitude of Baton Rouge; the lands lying south of this line being better adapted for sugar-cane than cotton, though even here cotton planters make a profitable investment in the raising of cotton. The general average of cotton crops, previous to the rebellion, was from eight to ten bales of cotton to the hand, and sometimes a dozen; the bales averaging four hundred pounds—and sugar-cane averaging two hogsheads of sugar and four barrels of molasses to the acre. The land as a general thing produced from twenty-five to forty bushels of corn per acre. Cotton on the plantation generally averaging from eight to ten cents per pound; and so abundantly was corn produced, that it scarcely received any notice in the scale of revenue except as an article of food for the hands and stock. Under the low prices of cotton, previous to the rebellion, a good hand, hired for the year, usually brought from two hundred to two hundred and fifty dollars, two suits of clothes, one blanket, and one pair of shoes, and board. From the high wages paid for labor and the low price of cotton, the planter who depended upon hired labor made but a poor investment of his capital compared with what he can now realize, from the high price of cotton and sugar; but we must not look for the same results now, as regards the amount of cotton produced by free labor in comparison with forced labor. The slave was seldom seen before sunrise at the house, nor before sunset, except on Sunday; and if he failed to plow the amount allotted, or hoe the number of rows in proper order, or fail to pick a certain number of pounds of cotton, wo betide him! Nor is it to be expected, that however industrious he may be, he can produce the same amount of labor. He is now a man of family; he has to take care of his children and find them the necessaries of life, which were attended to by his old master when a slave; besides, in case of sickness in his family, he has none to look to but himself; so, upon the whole, if the war had never broke out, and the negroes were freed, their social position, besides their improvidence, and idleness in a great many, would render it impossible to cultivate more than one half the lands, which would lie idle for lack of sufficient amount of labor to cultivate them.

We may now ask ourselves, what shall be done with the surplus lands? My answer is, whatever the old planter intends doing with them, he cannot afford to let them be idle. He must either sell or rent them. He cannot afford to let those lands lie idle, and pay three years' tax, he having paid none since the rebellion, in one payment; besides, he has to pay the usual tax imposed on the parish or county for county purposes. State taxes, and a tax he never paid before, and for which he never dreamed of having to pay when he was shouting hosannahs for Jeff. Davis and the Confederacy; *i. e.*, the internal revenue tax. Even, I say, however loth he may be to part with those lands, or have a "damned Yankee" for a neighbor, he sees there is no other resort left but to sell or rent his lands, or they have to be sold to pay the taxes.

There is another quality of lands of which I will take a brief notice: that is the creek lands, and small rivers in the interior. Upon all the water-courses, both in Louisiana and Texas, there are narrow strips of bottom land, on each side those rivers or creeks, on which chiefly reside the poorer classes of the Southerners, these lands have received little or no attention from the princely planter, they being generally in two [*sic*] small bodies to attract his notice. The lands on those creeks are notwithstanding very productive, and yield upon an average a bale of cotton to two acres, and from fifteen to twenty-five bushels of corn to the acre; besides, they are, after the first year's cultivation, easily cultivated; one hand can cultivate twenty acres with as little labor as he can ten on the Mississippi or bayous; besides, he has the advantage of good well and spring water, and an everlasting range for hogs and cattle, besides any amount of game. Those lands, with but few exceptions, are public lands, they not being rich enough, or in large bodies sufficient, to excite or attract the cupidity of the man of means.

In the State of Texas the facilities of obtaining lands is much easier than in Louisiana. The same causes which will induce the planter of Louisiana to rent or sell lands applies equally to the Texian planter. Many plantations are now entirely abandoned in Texas, or but partially occupied, having been abandoned since the cessation of hostilities; they being occupied and improved by those who abandoned their estates in Mississippi, Arkansas, and Louisiana, to escape with their negroes and stock from the invasion, to those States, of the Federal armies, have since, for the most part, gone back to their old homes; besides, there are millions of wood lands in Texas, being owned by speculators, who purchased large bodies of land with the view of selling them to the slave owner emigrant in large tracts, previous to the rebellion, it was next to an impossibility to buy a tract of one or two hundred acres from the land speculator; it being an arrangement which did not suit him to break into his calculations of disposing of large tracts to the wealthy slave owner, consequently the poor white man, in Texas, had to content himself the best he could, and make the best living he could off the pine lands and creek bottoms. But since the slave monopoly has been overthrown, the Texian speculator would be very glad to sell his lands upon the most reasonable terms. I would here remark that the speculators owned the best of the lands in Texas, as they had an opportunity of examining the kind of lands they entered previous to their purchasing them. And as their object was to sell those lands to those who raised cotton, you may rely upon it, those lands are not to be excelled for the production of that staple by any lands in the State.

Here is a broad field of operations, offered to the Northern farmer and capitalist, to make good and permanent homes and profitable investments for capital; nor is it to those alone this inducement is held out; the mechanic will find employment there in the erection of dwelling-houses, gin-houses, and sugar-houses, which have been destroyed during the war, or which fell into decay for lack of improvements and occupancy; wages now in Louisiana being, for mechanics, from $5 to $7 per day; whilst board is not as dear as it is in Washington.

As to the laboring man, I would say to him, by all means go South and earn for yourself a farm, which you can do by industry and perseverance in a few days, which you cannot do by manual labor in the North during your life-time.

You work upon public works, say at two dollars a day, which is the maximum wages of a laborer. Upon an average you do not work during the year, perhaps, over twenty days in the month, whilst for board and lodging you pay twenty-five dollars per month, leaving you but fifteen dollars clear. But you do not clear this much, for you have to pay for washing, tobacco, and other little expenses, which you will find as a draw-back on your monthly wages; so, by the end of the year you have not enough left to buy yourself a decent suit of clothes; and the result of your year's labor is that your expenses have eaten the proceeds of your labor, leaving you, perhaps, a month or two indebted to your boarding-house, and which, if you are an honest man, you will again have to go to work and earn money to pay your board bill, and this brings you to commence the same routine of labor and indebtedness *ad infinitum;* whilst a laboring man in the South, upon a farm, gets from twenty to twenty-five dollars per month, board, lodging, and washing; and as the climate is mild, he needs but very light clothing to keep him comfortable, and those of a coarse, strong material. He is now in the country; he has no need to go finely dressed except on Sundays; he has not the thousand and one inducements in the country to spend his money which he has in the cities; and should he hire his time for a part of the crop, which is most frequently the case, he will have, in two years, the nucleus upon which he can start a little farm "on his own hook."

Such are my views respecting the enterprise upon which your society has embarked; and as I see your object is not to be a benefit to the stockholders of the United States Mutual Protection Company only, but a benefit and an everlasting blessing to the needy and industrious, who, when after a few years of trial in their new field of operation, will in the sincerity of their hearts call down innumerable blessings upon the company, and all who aided and assisted them in this most laudable enterprise.

I remain, sir, very respectfully,
your obedient servant,
D. E. HAYNES.

EXTRACTS FROM THE JOURNAL OF C. S. G. CLIFTON, A. M.,

Formerly Sergeant Major 2nd U.S. Cavalry, and a Returned Refugee.

July, 1865.—Having received information that my two sons were on their way home from the war, I immediately embarked on board the steamer Elenor, at New Orleans, for Alexandria. In a very few days I arrived at Alexandria, late in the night, with my two trunks of clothing; with no small trouble obtained lodging for the remainder of the night. Early next morning, seeing an ox-team in town—the men with it were residents of Bundic's [*sic*] creek, Calcasieu parish, about eighty-five miles distant—hoping to see or hear from my younger children, I succeeded in putting my trunks on board of their wagon, to accompany them out for the pine woods. About half way on the route, I heard my children had gone to some remote parts of Texas, and, at the solicitation of one of the men with us, I walked the entire distance to Bundic's creek settlement for the purpose of obtaining a school. The school could have been obtained, but a difficulty in the way of making payment presented as an obstacle. I next learned my children had returned from Texas, were at Sugar Town, and my eldest daughter sick and at the point of death.

I now had to leave my clothing at Bundic's creek, and walk eighteen or twenty miles to Sugar Town, where I found my three children;

the eldest girl, apparently on her death-bed, in an uncomfortable, ragged, and starving condition—no parent, no home—like poor, distressed little creatures expecting to be bound out at short notice. All we possessed was taken; their house burnt up by "Bloody Bob's" guerrillas or cavalry. Distressed in mind, I walked a long distance for medical aid; as for medicine we had none. In a very few days my daughter got a little better, and by a plea of mercy I succeeded in getting the children removed to an old school house. From this on it appears that nothing but disaster upon disaster followed us. As for my clothing—and it was some time before my trunks could come to Sugar Town—I had to sell it at the following sacrifice: a fine broadcloth dress coat, that cost forty-five dollars in New Orleans, for a three-year old beef, worth ten or fifteen dollars; dress waistcoat, worth eight dollars, for six hundred ears of corn; and so on with every other article—for the children had to subsist, as a matter of course.

Next, as soon as circumstances would permit, I walked, in warm weather, sixty-five miles to Alexandria, with my papers, hoping to receive from the United States Government some assistance, inasmuch as I had periled my life in defence of the same. The much-needed assistance I did not receive, although my children were ragged, starving, and without a home. I got a few quarter rations, say about fifteen pounds of pork and twelve pounds of hard bread. But then there were ten or twelve persons to have transportation with that ox-wagon; so, to be brief, on my return, as the children's rations had to be cooked for support on the road, they only had about eighteen crackers and one pound of pork remaining. I merely mention this in order to show the trouble I had to support them. I now had to cast about in double-quick time to see what next could be done, as the times here were so very pressing, and self-interest was the order of the day; in other words, there were people living around us who cared nothing for who sunk, if they only could swim. I recollected I had a little improvement at Six Mile creek that, peradventure, the cavalry had not burned. To that I proposed to the children we should go; but, having no team, how to get there was the question, and none could be hired on any terms;

well, as we had not much of this world's store left, we, at different times, carried it there. Having made the second trip, and returned the distance of eight miles, on our return with the balance of the children's effects, we found some evil-disposed persons had thrown part of the roof off our dwelling-house, so as to effectually fill the bill—out of the frying-pan into the fire.

Our row was now hard indeed; however, I hired a man to help me fix it again. Next, having received a letter from an old Mississippi neighbor, who now lived a long way down in Calcasieu parish, on Hickory Branch, stating they would be happy of my services as a teacher, and if I accepted of a school there he would come with an ox-team for us. With no small trouble we again removed to the old school house at Sugar Town, thinking it would shorten his distance some eight miles, the weather being very warm; we waited two weeks, on bread and water expenses, and still he came not. By solicitation embarked in a small school at this place, at two dollars in money or two fifty in corn or produce per scholar per month. Some that signed failed to send; all had more or less excuse; eventually, however, one employer sent two scholars, and advanced ten bushels of corn for two months only, which I received and stored at his crib, thinking, perhaps, the children might now have bread at least for a short time; as for water, we could obtain that free of cost; but fate and fortune, it appears, had another difficulty in store for us. Hardly three weeks of the quarter session had gone into operation, when a return of some of our former neighbors was announced in the settlement. One of them was a school mistress. On a sudden I was notified to get another place, as this old lady was about to commence a large school, on very reduced terms, at the house my children occupied. Here was another obstacle now to combat with, and the signer of two for two months now wanted his corn back again. Well, for a brief conclusion, we now had to remove back again at a late season of the year to Six Mile, carrying only a small portion, about perhaps one bushel of grain, with us, and no way of getting to mill, and in immediate want of every necessary article. How we came out the sequel will show. We encamped that night, on

Six Mile, at the remains of what had once been our house, for the boards were thrown off the roof, and next morning, after having partaken of some bread and water, returned to an unoccupied house at Sugar Town, where we could obtain water; and the next suggestion was to move to Alexandria, in order to get more readily some employment for future support. I succeeded in getting provisions sufficient to carry us there, and a young man, going with an ox-team to embark in hauling freight, proffered to take us; we rolled on, nothing very material occurring, until we encamped a short distance the other side of Ten Mile creek, and could have reached Alexandria in two more days' travel; unfortunately for us, the young man meeting his uncle and team, who had been there hauling freight and now loaded for home, prevailed on him to return; accordingly we were left on the road to travel the balance of the way as best we could. This was now another serious difficulty for myself and three unfortunate children to contend with. As our little supply of provisions was now fast diminishing, it required no small casting about to ascertain what next should be done in order to get a team; all the teams in this neighborhood were employed, and but few, if any, wagons passing; our row was now hard indeed—fifty miles from shore and no pole to touch bottom—we were informed, however, that a team was expected to pass in course of one or two days at the furthest, but whether we could obtain transportation aboard that or not was the now all-important question; well, Saturday passed, Sunday came, and is apparently passing without signs of the ox-team appearing. How we shall ever yet come out of present difficulty the balance of this journal must determine. Walked forty-three miles, going and returning, to try to hire a team to transport us; the children's provision rapidly diminishing; no less than fourteen applications for a team—they are all employed and none to be had on any terms—the promise of one, however, next Friday; my eldest daughter still very feeble, and more or less chill and fever, and my own health on the decline. What next is to follow time alone can tell. But we hope yet to get on, and find employ for future support. Arrived at Alexandria, received a few rations, and, through the influence of the provost marshal and very polite letter of recommendation to the quartermaster, obtained employ with the United States Government as forage master. The monthly pay and rations being good, for which we are extremely thankful, we hope the present dark cloud will pass away, and awaken to rise on brighter prospects for the future.

THE END.

NOTES

Editor's Introduction

1. Tommy Haynes to the editor, April 13, 1999; Mary B. Erickson to the editor, April 16, 1999; "Report of the Joint Committee on Reconstruction," Part IV, Report No. 30, *House Reports*, 39th Congress, 1st Session, 1865–1866, 59; *New Orleans Times*, March 2, 1864; Population Schedules, Seventh Census, 1850, Lee County, Georgia, National Archives.

2. James E. and Josiah Wheat, *Sketches of Tyler County History* (Bevil Oaks, Tex.: Whitmeyer Printing, 1986), 85; Population Schedules, Eighth Census, 1860, Rapides Parish, Louisiana, and Tyler County, Texas; Record of Dennis E. Haynes, Compiled Service Records of Volunteer Union Soldiers Who Served in Organizations from the State of Louisiana, Microcopy No. 396, Roll 11, National Archives, hereinafter cited as C.S.R.; Deposition by Dennis E. Haynes, August 19, 1873, in *Dennis E. Haynes v. United States*, U.S. Court of Claims, Congressional Jurisdiction Case #1745, Dennis E. Haynes, Box 298, 16E3/8/28/1, Record Group No. 123, National Archives.

3. Haynes Deposition, August 19, 1873, in *Dennis E. Haynes v. United States.*

4. C.S.R. of Haynes; "Report of the Joint Committee," 60–61; D. E. Haynes, Box 13, U.S. Treasury Department, Records of the Secretary, Subseries 247e, Record Group 56, National Archives.

5. Alexander P. Field to Hon. H. L. Dawes, December 1, 1865, D. E. Haynes, Box 11, Series 258, Applications for Assessor, 2nd District, Louisiana, Record Group 56, National Archives.

6. Marriage Records Transcribed, Book 2 & 3, 83, 94, 176; Burrell Phillips and Permilia Dean to Patrick Haynes, January 4, 1883, Deed Record M, 5–7, Tyler County Courthouse, Woodville, Texas.

7. T. Harry Williams, *Huey Long* (New York: Alfred A. Knopf, 1969), 10–11, 14–15; Tax Assessment Roll, Winn Parish, 1869, Louisiana State Archives and Records Service; Population Schedules, Ninth Census, 1870, Winn Parish, Louisiana; Conveyance Book "T," 356–57, Winn Parish Courthouse, Winnfield, Louisiana.

8. *Dennis E. Haynes v. United States.*

9. Haynes Deposition, August 19, 1873, in *Dennis E. Haynes v. United States;* "Resolutions &c., adopted at a meeting of the Republican party of Winn

Parish," October 7, 1871, Letters Received, Superintendent of Education, 1865–1877, Louisiana State Archives; Appointment Book, Grant Parish Courthouse, Colfax; Tax Assessment Rolls, Winn Parish, 1870–1875. The aforementioned deposition is the latest date for which the editor has found a record for Haynes.

10. Marriage Records, Book 2 & 3, 166, 242; Deed Record H, 286–87; Deed Record I, 21–22, 244; Deed Record J, 79, Tyler County Courthouse.

Chapter 1

1. Major General Richard Taylor's small Confederate army retreated from its position at Fort Bisland on Bayou Teche when outflanked by the Union army under Major General Nathaniel P. Banks on April 13, 1863. The Confederate army fell back first to Opelousas, which they abandoned April 19 in the face of superior numbers, and later to Alexandria. U.S. War Department, *War of the Rebellion: Official Records of the Union and Confederate Armies*, 128 parts in 70 vols. (Washington, D.C.: Government Printing Office, 1880–1901), Series 1, Vol. XV, 388–94, hereinafter cited as *O.R.*, all citations are to Series 1 unless otherwise stated.

2. The Eleventh Texas Infantry Battalion, Lieutenant Colonel Ashley W. Spaight, was made up of men from Jasper, Newton, Orange, Jefferson, Tyler, Hardin, Chambers, and Liberty counties in southeast Texas. Companies C, D, and E received orders to report to Taylor in Louisiana and left Galveston on May 9, 1863. Cooper K. Ragan (ed.), "The Diary of Captain George W. O'Brien, 1863," *Southwestern Historical Quarterly* 67 (1963): 30–31, 45; *O.R.*, XV, 1071.

3. No specific information of these meetings has been found.

4. Josiah Phelps was a thirty-four-year-old farmer born in Louisiana. Population Schedules, Eighth Census, 1860, Hardin County, Texas.

5. The town of Hardin was the county seat of Hardin County.

6. Joe Adams has not been identified.

7. George W. Van Vleck of Woodville had been district clerk of Tyler County. He was born in New York in 1815. As a brigadier general, Van Vleck commanded the Second District, Texas State Troops, which included Chambers, Liberty, Polk, Tyler, Hardin, Jefferson, Newton, Jasper, and Orange counties. Population Schedules, Eighth Census, 1860, Tyler County, Texas.

8. Banks's army evacuated Alexandria May 14–15, 1863, having occupied the town only about a week, and marched to Simmesport to begin a movement against Port Hudson. Union forces advancing from Baton Rouge began skirmishing with the Confederates at Port Hudson on May 21, but Banks's army did not arrive and complete the investment of the Confederate garrison until May 23. *O.R.*, XXVI, Pt. 1, 12–13.

9. Lazarus Goolsby has not been identified.

10. Henry Barrington has not been identified.

11. Austin Presswood was a thirty-six-year-old farmer who was born in Georgia. Population Schedules, Eighth Census, 1860, Rapides Parish, Louisiana.

12. Taylor reported that during the retreat of his army from Fort Bisland most of the men of the Yellow Jacket (Tenth) Louisiana Infantry Battalion deserted to their homes in St. Martin Parish. Lieutenant Colonel Valsin A. Fournet mounted the remnant of his battalion on orders from Taylor to move against the Jayhawkers and deserters in western Rapides Parish. *O.R.*, XV, 393; John Dimitry, "Louisiana," *Confederate Military History*, ed. Clement A. Evans, 10 vols. (Atlanta: Confederate Publishing Co., 1899), X, 582.

13. James Parker, born in 1852, was the son of Isaiah and Dicey Ann Parker. Population Schedules, Eighth Census, 1860, Rapides Parish, Louisiana.

14. Benjamin F. Parker, the eighteen-year-old son of Isaiah and Dicey Ann Parker, was born in Mississippi. Population Schedules, Eighth Census, 1860, Rapides Parish, Louisiana.

15. Bob Flyn has not been identified.

16. Lieutenant Colonel Valsin A. Fournet resigned June 10, 1863, citing gout as the cause of his inability to continue on active duty. Record of Fournet, C.S.R., Microcopy 320, Roll 225, National Archives.

Several slightly different versions of the orders to the Yellow Jacket Battalion exist. One book indicates that there were actually two sets of orders, and the editor has chosen to quote that book as the most accurate source:

> Headquarters, Forces South of Red River,
> Vermillionville, La., June 15 [12?], 1863.
> General Orders, No.—
>
> Information has been received that there are bands of outlaws, deserters, conscripts and stragglers from a parish above Hineston, on the Calcasieu River, in the parish of Rapides, down to the lower parishes, extending into the parish of Calcasieu, through to the Bayou Teche, which are committing depredations, robberies, and incendiarism, and who are openly violating the Confederate laws, with arms in their hands. Such men can only be considered as outlaws, highwaymen and traitors.
>
> In consequence:
>
> I. You will proceed with your battalion up to the Calcasieu River, and in the vicinity of Hineston, in the parish of Rapides, and from that point scour the whole country, to the limit of Calcasieu parish, if to the Bayou Teche, in search of these outlaws, highwaymen and traitors. These bands, beyond the pale of society, must be exterminated especially the leaders; and every man found with arms for the purpose of

resisting the operations of the Confederate laws, or against whom satisfactory evidence may be given, must be executed on the spot.

No prisoners should be taken. Such as are not sufficiently guilty to demand immediate execution, must be liberated, and, if conscripts, ordered to report forthwith. Men by the names of Wittington, Elliot, Ozime, Carriere, Huddleston, have been designated as some of the ringleaders.

By order of
Brigadier General Alfred Mouton.
[Signed.] Louis Bush, Assistant
Adjutant General.

To Major G. A. Fournet Commanding Yellow Jacket Battallion:

These instructions are to be kept secret, and no one is allowed to know the objects of your movements, except yourself.

True copy. [Signed.] Louis Bush,
Assistant Adjutant General.
Lieut. G. J. DeBlanc, Acting Adjutant.

Headquarters, Forces South of Red River,
Vermillionville, La., June 15, 1863.

. Special Orders, No.—

In addition to the special instructions given you in orders bearing date the 12th instant, the following instructions are added for your guidance, viz:

I. All dissaffected persons, jayhawkers, etc., caught with arms, or proven to have been in arms against the Confederate authorities, should be shot without delay on the spot, when taken. No prisoners are to be taken from among the ringleaders of the gang.

II. In cases not covered by the above paragraphs when you have reason to believe that the parties are concerned in connection with any of these gangs, but entertain a reasonable doubt as to the guilt of these parties, you will hold them in close arrest, and report the case to Headquarters with such evidence as may exist.

III. No prisoners, except those mentioned, should be taken. Such as are not sufficiently guilty to deserve punishment, must be liberated, and, if conscripts, ordered to report to Camp Pratt, forthwith, with the injunction, that if you overtake them again, they will be executed on the spot.

IV. The object of your mission, as explained in previous orders, is to break these gangs of outlaws, robbers, and jayhawkers, and to execute all those found in arms, and especially the ringleaders. It has, besides, in view, to force all conscripts, if necessary, by compulsion and force of arms.

V. You will from time to time report to Headquarters giving full details of your operations.

By order of
Brigadier General Alfred Mouton.
[Signed.] Louis Bush, Assistant
Adjutant General.

To Major G. A. Fournet Commanding Yellow Jacket Battallion:

These instructions are to be kept secret. No one is allowed to know the object of your movements, except yourself.

[Signed.] Louis Bush, Assistant
Adjutant General.
True copy. Lieut. G. J. DeBlanc,
Acting Adjutant.

Elias P. Pellet, *History of the 114th Regiment, New York State Volunteers* (Norwich, N.Y.: Telegraph & Chronicle Power Press Print, 1866), 184–186. See also *Harper's Weekly,* December 19, 1863, and New Orleans *Era,* November 21, 1863, for variations of one or both of these orders.

17. Captain Davis has not been identified. Walker's Texas Infantry Division occupied Camp Texas about twenty miles southwest of Alexandria from August 10 to 30, 1863. Norman D. Brown (ed.), *Journey to Pleasant Hill: The Civil War Letters of Captain Elijah P. Petty, Walker's Texas Division, C.S.A.* (San Antonio: Institute of Texan Culture, 1982), 245, 249.

18. Alfred Wetherford was a sixty-year-old farmer born in South Carolina. Population Schedules, Eighth Census, 1860, Rapides Parish, Louisiana.

19. Francis Van Scarbrock was a forty-year-old farmer born in Belgium. Population Schedules, Eighth Census, 1860, Rapides Parish, Louisiana.

20. Haynes's activities in Nicaragua under William Walker are mentioned in the Editor's Introduction.

21. Mary Jane Nichols, twenty-nine years old in 1860, was the wife of Simon C. Nichols, a forty-three-year-old farmer. Population Schedules, Eighth Census, 1860, Rapides Parish, Louisiana.

22. Dr. A. P. Dudley, said to have been a physician in Calcasieu Parish when the war started, evaded conscription and organized a band of Jayhawkers, who later became scouts for the Union army. A correspondent wrote, "Many of the scouts are desperate men, who have suffered all manner of outrage at the hands of the enemy, and who, on this account, lose no opportunity to inflict the heaviest punishment on those who have driven them to the shelter of the swamps and forests. Captain Dudley is described as a slight, wiry man, about forty-five years old, with a small eye which is all black and a face which strikes one as full of cunning." *Harper's Weekly,* May 7, 1864.

23. Haynes here makes an error according to what he says elsewhere in his "Narrative." Jacob Gunter killed Dudley. The Green to whom he refers was

Uriah Green, paroled as a member of Company D, Seventh Louisiana Cavalry Regiment, at Washington, Louisiana, on June 17, 1865. Green supposedly killed Jayhawker leader Ozeme Carriere. File of Onezime Matte, Confederate Pension Applications, Louisiana State Archives and Records Service; C.S.R., M320, Roll 24.

24. Robert Washington Martin, a farmer born in Georgia, formed a company of home guards which entered Confederate service November 1, 1863. The unit later became Company K, Sixth Louisiana Cavalry Regiment. Population Schedules, Seventh Census, 1850, Sabine Parish, Louisiana; C.S.R., M320, Roll 23; Capt. A. H. May to Capt. W. H. Harrison, January 23, 1864, Letters Sent Book, District of West Louisiana, January–February 1864, Ch. II, Vol. 75, 101, Record Group 109, War Department Collection of Confederate Archives, National Archives. Martin left Louisiana shortly after the end of the war and settled near Mooreville in Falls County, Texas. He may have feared revenge for his wartime actions. His family reported that he died there on November 13, 1866. This was the day when his wife gave birth to their last child. According to family members, Martin's friends knew that Federal soldiers might come looking for him some day and had promised to alert him if any troops came into the area. He decided to commit suicide rather than face hanging and shot himself in the face. The soldiers were shown his freshly dug grave. One descendant, Sherry Bob Merritt, speculates that he faked his death and may even have assumed an alias. As one strong clue that Martin did not die in 1866, she points to an 1897 roster of Company D, First Louisiana Cavalry Regiment, that appears in Howell Carter, *A Cavalryman's Reminiscences of the Civil War* (New Orleans, La.: American Printing Co., Ltd., 1900), 145. It shows that R. W. Martin was one of a number of soldiers "said to be living last year [1896]." Sherry Bob Merritt to the editor, April 19 and 20, 2004.

25. Levy Boyd was a twenty-eight-year-old farmer born in Mississippi. Population Schedules, Eighth Census, 1860, Rapides Parish, Louisiana. Wesley Lovin was probably J. W. Loving. He and Bryant Presley later served in the First Louisiana Battalion Cavalry Scouts. C.S.R., M396, Roll 11.

26. William W. Smart was a twenty-six-year-old overseer born in Louisiana and had represented Rapides Parish in the secession convention. Population Schedules, Eighth Census, 1860, Rapides Parish, Louisiana; *Biographical and Historical Memoirs of Northwest Louisiana* (Nashville, Tenn.: Southern Publishing Co., 1890), 283. Dr. E. E. Smart, a twenty-seven-year-old physician and farmer, had served in the state legislature as a representative and senator from Rapides Parish. Population Schedules, Eighth Census, 1860, Rapides Parish, Louisiana; *Biographical and Historical Memoirs*, 283. Reese W. Smart was a merchant born in Mississippi. Population Schedules, Seventh Census, 1850, Rapides Parish, Louisiana.

27. James P. Groves was a twenty-one-year-old farmer born in Louisiana

who served as a private in Company K, Sixth Louisiana Cavalry. Population Schedules, Eighth Census, 1860, Rapides Parish, Louisiana; C.S.R., M320, Roll 22.

28. George A. Smith had served as a lieutenant in a home guard company organized May 25, 1861, and commanded by Captain John P. Eddleman. No record of his service in Martin's company exists. *Biographical and Historical Memoirs of Northwest Louisiana*, 537.

29. Governor James Madison Wells appointed Smith as constable for the Anacoco ward of Rapides Parish. Alexandria *Louisiana Democrat*, October 18, 1865.

30. Mr. Walley has not been identified.

31. Mr. Lovin has not been identified.

32. Probably Augustus Clark, a thirty-one-year-old wheelwright. Population Schedules, Eighth Census, 1860, Rapides Parish, Louisiana.

33. Elijah Connelly's name was not found on the 1860 census for Rapides Parish.

34. The large number of men named Bass in Rapides Parish makes identification of this individual impossible.

35. Wells's summer house was called Jessamine Hill and was located in the pine woods a few miles south of Lecompte. He frequently hid in the nearby woods to escape Confederate soldiers and sympathizers who were chasing him. More often, Wells took refuge at his large hunting ground, Bear Wallow, near the Calcasieu River. George M. G. Stafford, *The Wells Family of Louisiana and Allied Families* (Alexandria, La.: Standard Printing Co., Inc., 1941), 98, 99; Walter M. Lowrey, "The Political Career of James Madison Wells," *Louisiana Historical Quarterly* 31 (1948): 1007.

36. Captain Samuel M. Todd commanded the Prairie Rangers, which became Company K, Third Louisiana Cavalry. Todd had known Wells prior to the war, and when he heard of the orders issued in November 1863 to arrest Wells, "he secretly sent word by a Negro servant to the accused man" so that he could escape. Todd deserted and turned himself in to Federal troops near Grand Ecore on April 5, 1864, saying "that he should now take the amnesty oath and try to get a job as a clerk in some department." Lowrey, "The Political Career of James Madison Wells," 1008–1009; Lawrence Van Alstyne, *Diary of an Enlisted Man* (New Haven, Conn.: Tuttle, Morehouse & Taylor Co., 1910), 301. With Wells's recommendation, Todd gained appointment by the president as registrar of the land office at Opelousas. Opelousas *Courier*, August 26, 1865.

37. As Wells saw the war coming to an end, he decided to adopt a conciliatory attitude toward the ex-Confederates and Confederate sympathizers. Wells's biographer wrote, "Believing that most of the Confederates had been seduced from their allegiance to the United States by the wiles of the 'demagogues' who brought on the rebellion, he '. . . determined to try the effect of

kindness and conciliation in weaning them back to their first love.'" Other factors behind his appointments were his desire to protect Louisiana "from the outrages of the political adventurers from the North" and his disagreement with the radical stance followed by his predecessor, Michael Hahn, who favored citizenship and voting rights for blacks. Lowrey, "The Political Career of James Madison Wells," 1024–25, 1033, 1039.

CHAPTER 2

1. Jacob Gunter was a twenty-nine-year-old farmer. He enlisted in Captain Todd's Prairie Rangers company and was mustered into Confederate service November 1, 1862, at Alexandria. According to Haynes's testimony before a congressional committee, Gunter joined Captain Alexander Strother's company of Louisiana Scouts. He returned to Confederate service and received his parole on June 14, 1865, as a member of Company K, Third Louisiana Cavalry. Population Schedules, Eighth Census, 1860, Rapides Parish, Louisiana; "Report of the Joint Committee," 61; C.S.R., M320, Roll 14.

2. Conflicting information exists on Dudley's fate. A contemporary newspaper account states that Confederate soldiers captured Dudley. In a letter to his wife, a Confederate officer stationed in Opelousas wrote that Dudley had been killed between December 29, 1864, and January 29, 1865. Citizens in Rapides Parish credited Lieutenant David C. Paul, Company G, Second Louisiana Cavalry, as Dudley's killer. *Opelousas Courier*, January 28, 1865; Bell I. Wiley (ed.), *"This Infernal War": The Confederate Letters of Sgt. Edwin H. Fay* (Austin: University of Texas Press, 1958), 419; Citizens to Maj. Gen. Simon B. Buckner, March 12, 1865, J. L. Brent Papers, Louisiana Adjutant General's Library, Jackson Barracks, New Orleans, hereinafter cited as Brent Papers, LAGL.

3. Probably Captain Charles H. Jones of Company K, Thirteenth Texas Cavalry (Dismounted) Regiment. He was a merchant in Woodville, Tyler County, when the war began. The 1860 Census gives his age as twenty-six and his birthplace as Tennessee. Jones served in the Texas legislature in 1866 and was an active Mason. He died in Woodville on August 23, 1880, and was buried in Magnolia Cemetery. *Members of the Texas Legislature, 1846–1962* (Austin: Legislature of the State of Texas, 1962), 54; Population Schedules, Eighth Census, 1860, Tyler County, Texas.

4. On February 6, 1863, the War Department authorized Captain Patrick F. Keary of Cheneyville to go from Virginia to western Louisiana and raise a battalion of sharpshooters for service with General Robert E. Lee's army. Keary and four lieutenants, all from Rapides Parish, reached Alexandria about March 17 and began recruiting shortly afterward. Banks's raid in May caused a temporary cessation of recruiting. On June 25, Keary received orders to arrest conscripts in Rapides, Sabine, and Calcasieu parishes. His orders also

read: "Should Capt Keary encounter any men bearing arms for the purpose of resisting the execution of the Conscript Law he will at once have all such shot down and is especially directed to take no prisoners among the ring-leaders of the jayhawkers scattered through the country in which he will operate, but to have the same summarily executed." C.S.R. of Keary, M320, Roll 193.

5. This was Haynes's son William.

6. Patrick Keary, who married Jefferson Davis's niece Helen, owned a plantation near the border of Rapides and Avoyelles parishes, while his brothers Hugh M. and W. E. owned land in Avoyelles. Haynes probably refers here to Hugh M. Keary. Like many other planters in the area, the Kearys moved their slaves and many personal belongings to Texas, hopefully beyond the reach of the Federals. Solomon Northup, *Twelve Years a Slave*, ed. by Sue Eakin and Joseph Logsdon (Baton Rouge: Louisiana State University Press, 1968), 113 n.3.

7. Keary's men arrested Haynes on October 27, 1863. New Orleans *Times*, March 2, 1864.

8. General Edmund Kirby Smith commanded the Trans-Mississippi Department with headquarters in Shreveport. War Department, *War of the Rebellion: Official Records of the Union and Confederate Armies*, 128 parts in 70 vols. (Washington, D.C.: Government Printing Office, 1880–1901), Series 1, Vol. XV, 948, 1005, 1054, hereinafter cited as *O.R.*, all references are to Series 1 unless otherwise stated.

9. Carroll Jones was a forty-five-year-old mulatto planter who owned $13,000 in real estate and had a personal estate of $2,300. Population Schedules, Eighth Census, 1860, Rapides Parish, Louisiana.

10. Keary's orders to move his command to Shreveport dated from August 9, but the orders may have been delayed or his duties extended until November. C.S.R., M320, Roll 193.

11. Patrick J. Loftus had served as a sergeant in Keary's Company H, Eighth Louisiana Infantry, until July 1862. He received a wound on July 1 and went home on furlough. He was paroled at Shreveport on June 13, 1865. C.S.R., M320, Roll 194.

12. The American Party, nicknamed the Know-Nothings, was formed in Louisiana in 1854. Its membership consisted largely of former members of the Whig Party. In existence until 1860, the party was strongly anti-foreign, especially opposing the Irish in New Orleans. Perry H. Howard, *Political Tendencies in Louisiana* (Baton Rouge: Louisiana State University Press, 1971), 75–76.

13. Sergeant Lee has not been identified.

14. Archibald Smith was a thirty-seven-year-old farmer born in Louisiana. Population Schedules, Eighth Census, 1860, Rapides Parish, Louisiana.

15. Jerry Vanchaux was a thirty-seven-year-old farmer born in Belgium. Population Schedules, Eighth Census, 1860, Rapides Parish, Louisiana.

Chapter 3

1. William E. Ivey and associates had formed a company "for the protection of [their] homes and families from the violence of certain bands of lawless men" in October 1863. The company operated originally as a home guard unit under the control of the state but became Company I, Sixth Louisiana Cavalry Regiment, in early 1865. Thomas C. Manning to W. E. Ivey, October 26, 1863, Letters Sent, Adjutant General's Office, Louisiana Militia, 1862–1865, 188, Adjutant General's Library, Jackson Barracks; Special Order No. 46, Headquarters Louisiana Forces, Adjutant General's Office, November 5, 1863, Orders, Adjutant General's Office, Louisiana Militia, 174, Louisiana State Archives; C.S.R., M320, Roll 22.

2. W. W. Taylor served as first lieutenant and C. E. Graham as second lieutenant of Ivey's company. Isaac Sweat enlisted as a private in the company February 19, 1864. C.S.R., M320, Rolls 22 and 23. Roussou has not been identified. John J. Swann had enlisted in Company E, Consolidated Crescent Regiment, on January 28, 1863, at Alexandria; he was detached to the provost guard at Alexandria on February 13, 1864. No evidence of his association with Ivey's company has come to light. C.S.R., M320, Roll 379. Hop Swan may have been Appleton G. Swann, brother of John J., who was captured by the Federals in April 1864 while serving in Company G, Second Louisiana Cavalry Regiment. C.S.R., M320, Roll 13; File of Appleton G. Swann, Confederate Pension Applications, Louisiana State Archives.

3. Probably Sophia Boyd, who had sons named Leonard, James, and William. Population Schedules, Eighth Census, 1860, Rapides Parish, Louisiana.

4. Robert Bruce is said to have decided upon another attempt to conquer Scotland following six unsuccessful battles against the English after he watched a spider attempt "to swing itself from one beam in the roof to another, for the purpose of fixing the line on which it meant to stretch its web." Bruce determined to "'be guided by the luck which shall attend this spider.'" When it succeeded on its seventh try, he resolved "to try his own fortune; and as he had never before gained a victory, so he never afterwards sustained any considerable or decisive check or defeat." Walter Scott, *Tales of a Grandfather: Being the History of Scotland*, ed. Edwin Ginn (Boston: Athenaeum Press, 1885), 86–87.

5. This may have been M. Lynch, formerly First Lieutenant in Company B, Thirtieth Louisiana Infantry Regiment. C.S.R., M320, Roll 359.

6. Possibly Noah Cloud, a forty-five-year-old farmer. His father was Jeremiah Cloud, a seventy-one-year-old farmer. Population Schedules, Eighth Census, 1860, Rapides Parish, Louisiana.

7. Levi Pedro has not been identified.

8. C. Johnson and G. Johnson served as privates in Ivey's Company I, Sixth Louisiana Cavalry, and were paroled at Alexandria on June 9, 1865. C.S.R., M320, Roll 22.

9. Widow Bass has not been identified.

10. John Doyle has not been identified.

11. Nathaniel Sanders was a thirty-nine-year-old engineer born in South Carolina. He enlisted in Company I, Sixth Louisiana Cavalry, on February 19, 1864, and was paroled at Natchitoches on June 16, 1865, possibly as an officer in the company. Population Schedules, Eighth Census, 1860, Rapides Parish, Louisiana; C.S.R., M320, Roll 23.

12. Dr. William Farquhar was a forty-eight-year-old farmer, born in Ohio. He moved to Burr's Ferry in 1852 from Cincinnati. Four years later he moved to Sugartown and practiced there until 1864. At that time he moved to Choupique, where he died October 14, 1889. His son's name was George. Population Schedules, Eighth Census, 1860, Rapides Parish, Louisiana; Maude Reid, *Early Calcasieu Doctors, 1850–1912* (Lake Charles, La.: First National Bank, 1969), 4–5.

13. Ozeme Carriere, a twenty-nine-year-old farmer living on Bayou Mallet west of Opelousas, became one of the primary leaders of the Jayhawkers in southwestern Louisiana. Population Schedules, Eighth Census, 1860, St. Landry Parish, Louisiana.

14. Mr. Iles has not been identified; a number of men with this surname lived in the area.

15. Haynes's reference here is to one of the following individuals. Caswell F. Pollard, a sixty-year-old farm laborer born in Louisiana. Population Schedules, Eighth Census, 1860, Rapides Parish, Louisiana. John D. Pollard, a thirty-eight-year-old farm laborer born in Massachusetts and resident of Sugartown. Population Schedules, Eighth Census, 1860, Calcasieu Parish, Louisiana.

16. Green Pharris was a twenty-eight-year-old teamster living in Sugartown. Population Schedules, Eighth Census, 1860, Calcasieu Parish, Louisiana.

17. Paul Young was a twenty-five-year-old farm laborer of Sugartown. Population Schedules, Eighth Census, 1860, Calcasieu Parish, Louisiana.

18. Richard Burt was a thirty-eight-year-old farm laborer born in Massachusetts. Population Schedules, Eighth Census, 1860, Calcasieu Parish, Louisiana.

19. Located in present-day Allen and Beauregard parishes, Whiskey Chitto Creek gets its name from a Choctaw Indian word, "Uskichitto," which means "big cane."

20. Jones has not been identified.

21. William Simmons was a thirty-year-old farmer born in Mississippi. Population Schedules, Eighth Census, 1860, Rapides Parish, Louisiana.

22. .Ursin Carriere was a forty-six-year-old ferryman at Hickory Flat. Population Schedules, Eighth Census, 1860, Calcasieu Parish, Louisiana.

23. Beyham has not been identified.

24. The Federal army began evacuating Washington November 1 and had reached New Iberia by November 17. *O.R.*, XXVI, Pt. 1, 341, 346.

Chapter 4

1. The Federal army moved to Franklin between January 1 and 24, 1864. *O.R.*, XXXIV, Pt. 2, 158.

2. Private John McCormick, Company C, 114th New York Infantry Regiment. Harris H. Beecher, *Record of the 114th Regiment, N.Y.S.V.* (Norwich, N.Y.: J. F. Hubbard Jr., 1866), 549.

3. George C. Hubbard was commissioned assistant surgeon of the 165th New York Infantry on September 16, 1862. Frederick Phisterer (comp.), *New York in the War of the Rebellion, 1861 to 1865*, 5 vols. (Albany, N.Y.: I. B. Lyon Co., 1912), V, 3925.

4. James D. Blair was mustered in as captain of Company B, Second Louisiana Cavalry, in September 1862 and promoted to major of the regiment on January 14, 1863. C.S.R., M320, Roll 8.

5. Thomas J. Stafford was mustered in as captain of Company G, Second Louisiana Cavalry, on June 2, 1862, at Alexandria C.S.R., M320, Roll 13. A brother of Brigadier General Leroy A. Stafford, Thomas owned "Beaufort" plantation on the Red River southeast of Alexandria. George M. G. Stafford, *General Leroy Augustus Stafford: His Forebears and Descendants* (New Orleans, La.: Pelican Publishing Co., 1943), 181.

6. John O'Brien's name was not found on the 1860 census for Calcasieu Parish.

7. Josiah Johnson was a fifty-year-old farmer and Dempsey Iles a sixty-four-year-old farmer, both of Sugartown. Population Schedules, Eighth Census, 1860, Calcasieu Parish, Louisiana.

8. William A. Whittaker served as a lieutenant in the Second Louisiana Cavalry and was provost marshal at Vermillionville. C.S.R., M320, Roll 13.

9. James K. Beldon, then serving as mayor of Abbeville, was arrested by the Confederates on January 16, 1864, and taken to Vermillionville. He was accused of acting as a spy for the Federals. After a few days, the Confederates released him. One account said his release came because of his affiliation with the Masons, of which organization Colonel William G. Vincent of the Second Louisiana Cavalry was a member. The Confederates arrested Beldon again on January 25, and he had to walk with other prisoners to Alexandria. By February 27, he had returned home "*honorably acquited*." Priscilla M. Bond Diary, Louisiana and Lower Mississippi Valley Collection, LSU Libraries, Baton Rouge.

10. William G. Vincent assumed command of the Second Louisiana Cavalry as its colonel on September 1, 1862. C.S.R., M320, Roll 13.

11. Smith has not been identified.

12. Haynes received the following document upon his release:

> Office Provost Marshal,
> Vermillionville, La., Feb. 12th, 1864.
>
> Permission is hereby granted to John O'Brien to pass to the parish of Calcasieu (his home) upon his parole of honor that he will communicate nothing to the enemies of the Confederate States which, if known to them, would be injurious to the Confederate States.
>
> Wm. A. Whitaker,
> Lieutenant and Provost Marshal.
>
> This is to certify that John O'Brien was arrested by Major J. D. Blair, of 2d Regiment Louisiana Cavalry, in the town of New Iberia, on the 16th day of January, 1864, as a suspicious character, but after remaining in custody until this, the 12th day of February, 1864, at which time he is honorably released by orders of Col. Wm. G. Vincent, commanding 2d Regiment Louisiana Cavalry, and respectfully approved by myself.
>
> Wm. A. Whitaker,
> Lieutenant and Provost Marshal.

New Orleans Times, March 2, 1864.

Chapter 5

1. Captain Allen Jumel, Company I, Second Louisiana Cavalry. C.S.R., M320, Roll 10.

2. John S. Fitch was a forty-five-year-old carpenter born in New York. Population Schedules, Eighth Census, 1860, St. Landry Parish, Louisiana.

3. Captain T. Lytt Lyon, formerly of Company E, Crescent (Louisiana) Regiment, was serving as acting assistant commissary of subsistence. C.S.R., M320, Roll 384; *O.R.*, XXXIV, Pt. 2, 964.

4. Samuel D. Ashe was a forty-four-year-old planter born in South Carolina and had served as a colonel in the St. Landry Parish militia. Population Schedules, Eighth Census, 1860, St. Landry Parish, Louisiana.

5. The location of Peek's Ferry has not been ascertained.

6. Possibly John J. Burton, a twenty-year-old overseer at Cypress Point. Population Schedules, Eighth Census, 1860, Pointe Coupee Parish, Louisiana.

7. Possibly William Cutlett, a forty-year-old planter born in Georgia. Population Schedules, Eighth Census, 1860, Pointe Coupee Parish, Louisiana.

8. Possibly Victor Hebert, a fifty-five-year-old overseer on False River. Population Schedules, Eighth Census, 1860, Pointe Coupee Parish, Louisiana.

9. Haynes arrived at Port Hudson on Sunday, February 21, 1864. *New Orleans Times*, March 2, 1864.

Chapter 6

1. Andrew Jackson Hamilton received an appointment as brigadier general and military governor of Texas on November 14, 1862. He made a speech to Texas refugees at Lyceum Hall on the night of February 27, 1864. *O.R.*, 3, II, 782, 783; *New Orleans Times*, March 1, 1864.

2. S. N. Moody's Store was located at the corner of Canal and Royal streets. *New Orleans Times*, April 10, 1864.

3. E. A. Swearengen was a twenty-two-year-old merchant born in Georgia. Population Schedules, Eighth Census, 1860, Tyler County, Texas.

4. "A Personal Narrative—Escape of D. E. Haynes from Rebeldom" appeared in the *New Orleans Times* on March 2, 1864.

5. Wells had been elected lieutenant governor of the Union-controlled areas of the state on February 22, 1864. He and Governor Michael Hahn were inaugurated in New Orleans on March 4. Lowrey, "James Madison Wells," 1016.

6. Nothing is known of Dudley's background. He applied on February 17 in New Orleans to raise a squadron of cavalry scouts. A. P. Dudley to Brig. Gen. C. P. Stone, February 17, 1864, in File 2055Vs1872, First Louisiana Independent Cavalry Scouts, Record Group 94, Records of the Adjutant General's Office, 1780s-1917, Volunteer Service Branch, National Archives, hereinafter cited as File 2055Vs1872. James Madison Wells's brother Montfort intimated in a letter to a newspaper that Dudley had spent time with James Madison at his hunting camp, Bear Wallow, prior to Wells's escape from Confederates sent to arrest him in November 1863. Alexandria *Louisiana Democrat*, August 16, 1865.

7. Brigadier General Charles P. Stone received orders to report to New Orleans for assignment on May 7, 1863. He became chief of staff of the Department of the Gulf (Nineteenth Army Corps) on July 25, 1863. *O.R.*, XV, 719; XXVI, Pt. 1, 660.

8. Major General William B. Franklin had assumed command of the XIX Corps on August 15, 1863, and had commanded all troops in the field in south Louisiana during October and November of that year. *O.R.*, XXVI, Pt. 1, 340, 350, 684.

9. The Federal cavalry began its movement on March 14, 1864. The lead brigade was Colonel Nathan A. M. Dudley's Fourth Brigade, Cavalry Division, Department of the Gulf. *O.R.*, XXVI, Pt. 1, 444–45. Rev. James K. Ewer, *The Third Massachusetts Cavalry in the War for the Union* (Maplewood, Mass.: William G. J. Perry Press, 1903), 136.

10. Fort DeRussy, on the Red River near Marksville, fell to troops of the

Sixteenth Army Corps on March 14, 1864. Major General Andrew J. Smith led detachments of the Sixteenth and Seventh corps, which moved up Red River from the Mississippi River to join Banks at Alexandria. *O.R.*, XXXIV, Pt. 1, 305.

11. Louis Texada had served as one of Rapides Parish's three representatives in the secession convention. At the end of the war, he was paroled as Captain of Company D, First Louisiana Regiment Reserve Corps. *Official Journal of the Proceedings of the Convention of the State of Louisiana* (New Orleans, La.: J. O. Nixon, Printer to the State Convention, 1861), 10; C.S.R., M320, Roll 90.

A newspaper account stated that after taking the oath, Texada returned to his plantation unmolested by the Federal troops. In late April, a party of former Jayhawkers surrounded his house, possibly with a view to inflict some punishment for his activities in the secession convention. Texada escaped with the aid of his black servants and sought refuge within Federal lines in Alexandria. There "he received notice that he was a dangerous person, and must leave our lines. He said: 'I will not do it; if I go out I shall be hung by the Jay-Hawkers, and I will stay here in jail.'" New Orleans *Era*, May 4, 1864.

12. In his proclamation of December 8, 1863, President Abraham Lincoln provided for the readmission of Southern states whenever 10 percent of the people voting in 1860 took an oath of loyalty and after adoption of constitutions abolishing slavery. James D. Richardson, *A Compilation of the Messages and Papers of the Presidents, 1789–1902*, 10 vols. (Washington, D.C.: Bureau of National Literature and Art, 1903), VI, 213–15.

13. President Andrew Johnson's amnesty proclamation of May 19, 1865, was extended to all except persons who held high military or civilian positions in the Confederacy. Richardson, *A Compilation of the Messages and Papers of the Presidents*, 310–12.

14. Dissatisfied with Wells and the regular Democratic Party platform, reactionary Democrats placed the name of Confederate governor Henry W. Allen, then in exile in Mexico, on the ballot as a candidate for governor in the November 6, 1865, election. The election returns for Rapides Parish showed 347 votes for Allen and only 196 for Wells. Lowrey, "James Madison Wells," 1058, 1062.

15. On the night of March 22, 1864, Federal troops surrounded the Second Louisiana Cavalry and Captain William Edgar's Texas Battery at Henderson Hill, about twenty-two miles from Alexandria on Bayou Rapides, and captured 261 officers and men of the two commands. *O.R.*, XXXIV, Pt. 1, 307, 308.

16. Blair had received promotion to lieutenant colonel on January 13, 1864, upon the resignation of the officer then holding that position in the Second Louisiana Cavalry. C.S.R., M320, Roll 8.

17. A. K. Bevers, a forty-seven-year-old farmer born in St. Tammany Parish, enlisted on April 22, 1864, as first lieutenant in Company B, First Louisiana Battalion Cavalry Scouts. C.S.R., M396, Roll 11.

18. General Banks authorized the recruitment of a regiment of cavalry scouts for service with the Union army. Haynes raised a company of 118 men. Wells claimed that he raised eight companies of 40–60 men each for the regiment. *House Reports*, 39 Congress, 1 Session, No. 30, Pt. 4, 62; Lowrey, "James Madison Wells," 1018.

19. David R. Shannon, Company B, First Louisiana Battalion Cavalry Scouts. C.S.R., M396, Roll 11.

20. Josiah Chambers was a forty-year-old planter who lived south of Alexandria. His property was valued at $458,500 and his personal estate at $28,000. Population Schedules, Eighth Census, 1860, Rapides Parish, Louisiana.

21. Larkin D. Corley was a forty-three-year-old farmer born in Jones County, Georgia; Albert Hawthorne a farmer born in Georgia; and Charles H. Willett a thirty-five-year-old engineer born in Madison County, Ohio. Their companies became Companies C, D, and A, respectively, of the First Louisiana Battalion Cavalry Scouts. Population Schedules, Eighth Census, 1860, Rapides Parish, Louisiana; C.S.R., M396, Roll 11.

22. On February 18, 1864, Dudley received permission to raise a squadron of scouts "to operate in the woodland country of West Louisiana." The squadron would consist of two companies of one hundred men each. Dudley and his first company were mustered in at New Orleans on February 23; he became a captain, and his company initially numbered only nineteen men. On March 8, Dudley and his men received orders to report to General Franklin at Franklin. They reached General Franklin at Carrion Crow Bayou about March 18, and he sent them "to the Piney Woods to examine routes and see the refugees and conscripts said to be hiding there." Dudley reported to the Federal army at Alexandria on March 23, having "gathered 60 recruits." The next day orders assigned Dudley's company to Brigadier General Albert L. Lee's Cavalry Division. Stone to Dudley, February 18, 1864, in File 2055Vs1872; Para I, Special Order No. 48, Headquarters Department of the Gulf, February 23, 1864, in File 2055Vs1872; Para X, Special Order No. 59, Headquarters Department of the Gulf, March 8, 1864 File 2055Vs1872; Para I, Field Order No. 2, Headquarters Department of the Gulf, March 24, 1864, in File 2055Vs1872; *O.R.*, XXXIV, Pt. 1, 179; Pt. 2, 700, 714.

23. Brigadier General Cuvier Grover had been placed in command at Alexandria while the army marched toward Shreveport, and his Second Division, Nineteenth Corps, had remained to garrison the town. *O.R.*, XXXIV, Pt. 1, 198.

24. Wells was said to have promised in his recruiting speech that the men joining the Louisiana Scouts would receive a three-hundred-dollar bonus. Lowrey, "James Madison Wells," 1018.

25. The Federal army reached Alexandria on its retreat down Red River on April 25–26, 1864. *O.R.*, XXXIV, Pt. 1, 208.

26. Polk's Bridge crossed Bayou Lamourie near its junction with Bayou Boeuf south of Alexandria.

Chapter 7

1. The Federals evacuated Alexandria on May 13, 1864. While most sources state that the incendiaries cannot be identified positively, one Union soldier wrote, "The Jay-hawkers kept their promise to burn the place rather than have it go into the hands of the enemy again." Van Alstyne, *Diary of an Enlisted Man*, 320; *O.R.*, XXXIV, Pt. 1, 211.

2. Mrs. Clara Flowers owned a plantation on Bayou Rapides. At various times, both armies used her land as camping ground. Population Schedules, Eighth Census, 1860, Rapides Parish, Louisiana.

3. Major Henry F. Williamson was originally in the Second Louisiana (Union) Cavalry but went into the First Louisiana (Union) Cavalry when the units were consolidated on August 25, 1864. File 2055Vs1872; *Official Army Register of the Volunteer Force of the United States Army for the Years 1861, '62, '63, '64, '65* (Washington, D.C., 1865), 1156.

4. The retreating Federals burned the homes and other buildings of former governor Thomas O. Moore, Josiah Chambers, and other planters and farmers who lived along their route of march. G. P. Whittington, *Rapides Parish, Louisiana: A History* (Baton Rouge, La.: Franklin Press, Inc., n.d.), 191.

5. Gervais Baillio, formerly parish judge for Avoyelles Parish (1839–1846), owned Rosalie Plantation on Bayou Robert, south of Alexandria. He had served on the first Board of Supervisors of the Louisiana State Seminary of Learning and Military Academy (now Louisiana State University) and was a friend of William T. Sherman, first president of the school. Catherine Baillio Futch, *The Baillio Family* (Baton Rouge[?], 1961), 174, 177, 181.

6. The Confederates skirmished with the retreating Federals at Mansura on May 16, 1864, but were outflanked and forced to withdraw. *O.R.*, XXXIV, Pt. 1, 593.

7. Brigadier General Joseph A. Mower took three brigades of the Sixteenth Corps and fought a delaying action with the Confederates at Yellow Bayou on May 18, 1864, while the main army crossed the Atchafalaya River at Simmsport. After a sharp engagement both sides withdrew from the field. *O.R.*, XXXIV, Pt. 1, 320–21, 594.

8. The battle of Mansfield was also called the battle of Sabine Crossroads. Haynes's informant probably referred to the battles of Mansfield and Pleasant Hill, fought on April 8 and 9, 1864, respectively.

9. St. James Hospital, on Magazine Street between Natchez and Gravier streets, had been a hotel until taken over by Union major general Benjamin F. Butler in 1862. It had ten wards and four hundred beds. One report stated, "It

is one of the model hospitals of the department [of the Gulf]." New Orleans *Daily Picayune*, March 12, 1863; December 11, 1864.

10. Surgeon Lee has not been identified.

11. Elisha L. Brooks was quartermaster sergeant in Haynes's Company B, First Louisiana Battalion Cavalry Scouts. C.S.R., M396, Roll 11.

12. Colonel Daniel J. Keily commanded the Second Louisiana (Union) Cavalry. *Official Army Register*, 1156.

13. Major Juste Fontaine was appointed to the Second Louisiana (Union) Cavalry but never formally mustered in at that rank. *Official Army Register*, 1156.

14. Brigadier General William Dwight Jr. replaced Stone as Banks's chief of staff on April 17, 1864, but was relieved from that duty on June 29, 1864. *O.R.*, XXXIV, Pt. 3, 193; Pt. 4, 586.

15. The four companies of the First Louisiana Battalion Cavalry Scouts were consolidated with the Second Louisiana (Union) Cavalry as Companies H, I, K, and L on June 6, 1864. File 2055Vs1872; *Official Army Register*, 1156.

16. Both the Confederates and Federals, when they occupied New Orleans, used the large cotton presses as barracks.

17. Haynes, Corley, and Hawthorne were discharged on July 16, 1864, because of their ages. Major Williamson had recommended Haynes's discharge "for the benefit of the service" because he was "too old and otherwise entirely incompetent." Endorsement of Maj. Henry F. Williamson, June 16, 1864, on Capt. Dennis E. Haynes to Maj. G. B. Drake, June 1, 1864, in C.S.R., M396, Roll 11.

18. The Second Louisiana (Union) Cavalry was consolidated with the First Louisiana (Union) Cavalry August 25, 1864. Due to the dissatisfaction of the Louisiana Scouts with their placement in the Second Louisiana (Union) Cavalry, which resulted in a large number of desertions, and the subsequent consolidation of the two cavalry regiments, orders were issued on September 6 excluding the scouts from the consolidation. The order further stated: "These companies will be organized into a separate Battalion, for service in Western Louisiana, and Texas, in accordance with the articles of service in the original enlistment of the men." On October 12, the Union command issued new orders disbanding the Louisiana Scout battalion "in view of the reduced number of men fit for duty; of the fact that, from various causes, they are entirely without officers; and the irregularity attending their enlistment." The men received their muster out papers on November 12. Para III, Special Order No. 108, Headquarters Military Division of West Mississippi, August 25, 1864, in File 2055Vs1872; Para IV, Special Order No. 120, Headquarters Military Division of West Mississippi, September 6, 1864, in File 2055Vs1872, Para IV, Special Order No. 155, Headquarters Military Division of West Mississippi, October 12, 1864, in File 2055Vs1872; Adjt. Gen. E. D. Townsend to Secretary of War, May 22, 1872, in File 2055Vs1872.

19. An unidentified Texas cavalryman wrote the following from Trinity, on the Black River, on June 28, 1864: "The country through which we have journeyed since leaving Red River at Alexandria, is a high and dry pinny [*sic*] woods soil, worthless section, sparsely inhabited, and it would have been better for us if it was not inhabited at all. The people have been in the bushes sneaking nearly ever since the war commenced, and constantly conveying to the Yankees information that they acknowledge as being of a most valuable nature. Whilst Banks was in Alexandria they organized as a regiment of cavalry in the Yankee service, (to them the prisoners we took lay all the house burning, and everything else done contrary to civilized war,) and with them left the country. The commandant of the 'District of Western La.,' being desirous that they should not be separated from their families, took it into his head to rid the country of the stock, by sending out of our lines the families of the aforesaid traitors, consequently this country is indeed quite sparsely settled at this time. The last remnant of them crossed at this place but a few days ago on their way to Natchez, Miss." Galveston *Weekly News*, July 20, 1864.

20. Lieutenant David C. Paul, Company G, Second Louisiana Cavalry, commanded a squad of about thirty men who chased Jayhawkers in western Rapides, southern Sabine, and northern Calcasieu parishes from the fall of 1864 until the end of the war. C.S.R., M320, Roll 12; 31 citizens to Maj. Gen. Simon B. Buckner, March 12, 1865, Brent Papers, LAGL.

21. Joseph Benjamin raised a cavalry company of men from Rapides, Natchitoches, and Avoyelles parishes. The company entered Confederate service December 24, 1863. In February 1864, Benjamin received orders to take his company from Alexandria to operate with companies commanded by Captain William E. Ivey and Captain J. A. Weeks against Jayhawkers in western Rapides and southern Sabine parishes. Benjamin's company later served as the escort or headquarters company for the commander of the District of Western Louisiana. C.S.R., M320, Roll 30; Capt. A. H. May to Capt. J. A. Weeks, February 14, 1864, Letters Sent Book, District of West Louisiana, January–February 1864, Ch. II, Vol. 75, 239, RG 109, National Archives.

22. Several of the Jayhawker companies which organized as the Louisiana Scouts at Alexandria in April 1864 did not formally enter the Union army or leave the area when Banks's army retreated to the Mississippi River. Captain (or Major) Dudley, Captain Jerry Cloud, Captain Stanley, and Captain Alexander Strother all remained in the woods and swamps of western Louisiana with their companies. Several bands of Jayhawkers besides that of Ozeme Carriere continued to operate in southwestern Louisiana. At least one company, or band, of Jayhawkers returned to the swamps around Catahoula Lake. New Orleans *Era*, May 4, 1864; *Opelousas Courier*, October 22, 1864; unsigned statement, December 3, 1864, David F. Boyd Papers, Louisiana and Lower Mississippi Valley Collection, LSU Libraries, Baton Rouge; *O.R.*, XLVIII, Pt. 1, 1431.

23. Brigadier General John P. Hawkins was assigned to command the Western District of Louisiana with headquarters at Alexandria on July 20, 1865. *O.R.*, XLVIII, Pt. 2, 1094–95.

Chapter 8

1. The state constitution of 1864, ratified on July 23 of that year, was drawn up by white delegates from the parts of the state occupied by the Federals. In the document, slavery was abolished but blacks did not receive the right to vote. Under the document, elections were held for state and parish offices and a Union legislature to sit in New Orleans. Howard, *Political Tendencies in Louisiana*, 117–19.

2. Colonel Isaac F. Harrison commanded the Third Louisiana Cavalry Regiment, which operated primarily in the parishes bordering the west bank of the Mississippi River in north Louisiana. His men frequently chased conscripts, deserters, and Jayhawkers. C.S.R., M320, Roll 14.

3. On November 15, 1864, Thomas Jones of Vicksburg reported to Federal authorities that Captain Hedrick was at "Mrs. Moore's place, three miles south of Girard Station on the Shreveport and Texas Road, with sixty men. Captain Disharrom was on the [Bayou] Tensas, in Madison Parish, La., with a company of independent scouts thirty strong." *O.R.*, XLI, Pt. 4, 675. Captain Dishroom, or Disharrom, has not been identified. Captain Hedrick[s] may have been P. Headrick, an overseer near New Carthage. Population Schedules, Eighth Census, 1860, Madison Parish, Louisiana. S. A. Lusk was a scout and guide who frequently aided organized bodies of Confederate troops along the Mississippi River. He formed "a company which, when the scouting was done, was led always into the thickest of the fight." John N. Edwards, *Noted Guerrillas, or the Warfare of the Border* (St. Louis, Mo.: J. W. Marsh, 1880), 276–78.

4. Probably Captain Samuel Deweese, Company K, Sixty-sixth United States Colored Infantry. *Official Army Register of the Volunteer Force of the United States Army for the Years 1861, '62, '63, '64, '65*, 8 vols. and index (Washington, D.C.: Adjutant General's Office, 1865; reprint ed., Gaithersburg, Md.: Ron R. Van Sickle Military Books, 1987), Vol. VIII, 239.

5. E. D. Richardson and Charley Swan have not been identified.

6. Colonel Van E. Young, Forty-ninth United States Colored Infantry, commanded the Union post at Milliken's Bend as well as the First Brigade, First Division, United States Colored Troops. *O.R.*, XXXIX, Pt. 3, 69, 334, 464.

7. The Haynes child who died in New Orleans has not been identified but was probably a girl.

8. Colonel Samuel Thomas, Sixty-fourth United States Colored Infantry, was assigned on February 24, 1865, to inspect the affairs of freedmen in the Department of Misssissippi. *O.R.*, XLVIII, Pt. 1, 964.

9. Colonel Julian E. Bryant, Fifty-first United States Colored Infantry, was stationed at Milliken's Bend and assumed command of the post from Colonel Young, probably when Young became brigade commander. *O.R.*, XXXIX, Pt. 2, 334, 560.

10. The Forty-sixth United States Colored Infantry was one of the units assigned to the post at Milliken's Bend. *O.R.*, XXXIX, Pt. 2, 560.

11. Captain Robert G. Curtis served in several staff capacities at Vicksburg. *O.R.*, XLVIII, Pt. 1, 865.

12. Mr. Morea has not been identified.

13. Major General Napoleon J. T. Dana assumed command of the District of Vicksburg on August 7, 1864. *O.R.*, XLI, Pt. 2, 592.

14. George Clark has not been identified.

15. Mr. Parker has not been identified.

16. R. W. Graves was a fifty-six-year-old planter near Omega. Population Schedules, Eighth Census, 1860, Madison Parish, Louisiana.

17. Mrs. Susan Wells was a fifty-nine-year-old farmer near Omega. Population Schedules, Eighth Census, 1860, Madison Parish, Louisiana.

18. Samuel Barker was a thirty-seven-year-old planter near Omega. Population Schedules, Eighth Census, 1860, Madison Parish, Louisiana.

19. John Gyder was a twenty-seven-year-old cigar maker born in Baden, Germany. Population Schedules, Eighth Census, 1860, Madison Parish, Louisiana.

20. William S. Parham was a forty-year-old lawyer and planter born in Virginia. Population Schedules, Eighth Census, 1860, Madison Parish, Louisiana.

21. Mr. Cooper has not been identified.

22. Lieutenant Cheney has not been identified.

23. As stated, the Louisiana Scouts were disbanded in November 1864.

24. Confederate "partisans" had harassed the Federal lessees opposite Vicksburg so much through the waning months of 1864 that they had left more than one-third of the plantations in the area. Major General Edward R. S. Canby authorized the lessees in Carroll and Madison parishes "to organize a 600-man force to patrol and guard the plantations. Guns, ammunition, and rations for this group were furnished by the Government." James T. Currie, *Enclave: Vicksburg and Her Plantations, 1863–1870* (Jackson: University Press of Mississippi, 1980), 65–66.

25. Mr. McCullough has not been identified.

26. Mr. Watt has not been identified.

27. Lieutenant General Simon B. Buckner of the Confederate army signed terms of surrender of the Trans-Mississippi Department in New Orleans on May 26, 1865. The Federals did not consider the surrender official until Kirby Smith signed the terms, which he did at Galveston, Texas, on June 2. John D.

Winters, *The Civil War in Louisiana* (Baton Rouge: Louisiana State University Press, 1963), 426.

28. Mr. McCallister has not been identified.

Chapter 9

1. Brigadier General Jasper A. Maltby was assigned to command the Western District of Mississippi, with headquarters at Vicksburg, on July 17, 1865. *O.R.*, XLVIII, Pt. 2, 1087.

2. Major General Henry W. Slocum assumed command of the Department of Mississippi with headquarters at Vicksburg on July 14, 1865. *O.R.*, XLVIII, Pt. 2, 1078.

3. Thomas Montfort Wells, eldest son of James Madison, had served in the First Louisiana Cavalry Regiment in Tennessee but deserted in 1863. In 1865 he received an appointment as naval officer of the Port of New Orleans. George M. G. Stafford, *The Wells Family of Louisiana and Allied Families* (Alexandria, La.: Standard Printing Co., Inc., 1941), 106, 108.

4. Brigadier General Francis T. Sherman served as Provost Marshal of the Military Division of the Gulf. *O.R.*, XLVIII, Pt. 2, 1004–5.

5. Major General Philip H. Sheridan assumed command of the Military Division of the Gulf, with headquarters at New Orleans, on June 27, 1865. *O.R.*, XLVIII, Pt. 2, 1004.

6. See note 22 of chapter 7.

7. Possibly Anderson McNutt, a sixty-five-year-old farmer born in Virginia. Population Schedules, Eighth Census, 1860, Rapides Parish, Louisiana.

8. Possibly Hannah Perkins, a fifty-two-year-old farmer born in Louisiana. Population Schedules, Eighth Census, 1860, Rapides Parish, Louisiana.

9. Johnson has not been identified.

10. The Selonches and Dunhams have not been identified.

11. John Bogan Sr. was a fifty-year-old hotel keeper born in Ireland. His establishment was called the Rapides House. John Bogan Jr., twenty-eight years old, ran a coffee house. Population Schedules, Eighth Census, 1860, Rapides Parish, Louisiana; Walter Prichard (ed.), "A Tourist's Description of Louisiana in 1860," *Louisiana Historical Quarterly* 21 (1938): 1156.

12. Joseph W. Texada, a twenty-one-year-old planter, had been captain of Company A, Eighth Louisiana Cavalry Regiment. He received his parole at Alexandria on June 6, 1865. Population Schedules, Eighth Census, 1860, Rapides Parish, Louisiana; C.S.R., M320, Roll 26. Haynes claimed that, on September 4, 1865, he was "violently beaten" by Texada and saved from being murdered by the intervention of a friend. An Alexandria newspaper described the confrontation as "a fair fight with fists" in which Texada gave Haynes "a sound drubbing." The paper stated, "The cause of the assault was offensive con-

duct of Haynes to the ladies of Mr. Texada's family during the second raid [1864] of General Banks." Haynes failed in an attempt to have Texada prosecuted in Rapides Parish but succeeded in having Texada charged in United States District Court in New Orleans under the provisions of the Civil Rights Bill. In November 1869, Texada finally paid Haynes $250 for the injuries. Haynes to Maj. Gen. Philip H. Sheridan, May 25, 1866, in Haynes C.S.R., M396, Roll 11; *Louisiana Democrat*, July 4, 18, 25, 1866; Receipt, Dennis C. [*sic*] Haynes vs. Jos. W. Texada, dated November 3, 1869, Ker-Texada Papers, Manuscripts Department, Tulane University Archives, New Orleans. On May 21, 1866, Haynes wrote to Theodore "Dumps" Texada, Joseph's brother, saying, "Were it not for you Joe Texada would be rotting in his grave." Unfortunately, what he meant by this is unknown. Dennis E. Haynes to "Friend Texada," May 21, 1866, Texada Family Papers, 1855–1919, Tennessee State Library and Archives ("Friend Texada" was identified by a descendant of the family, Mary David Baker, in a communication to the editor, December 20, 2002).

13. J. H. C. Barlow announced his law practice in Alexandria in August 1865. *Louisiana Democrat*, August 9, 1865.

14. Captain James G. White had served as a judge advocate in the Trans-Mississippi Department. In August 1865, he opened a law office in the residence of R. M. Kilpatrick on 3rd Street in Alexandria and advertised that he would specialize in the settlement and collection of claims against the government. "Charges & specifications in case of John Droddy Private Co 'K' 3rd La Regt. Cavalry," January 5, 1865, Brent Papers, LAGL; *Louisiana Democrat*, August 30, 1865.

15. General George M. Graham was foreman of a grand jury empaneled by the district court on October 2, 1865. *Louisiana Democrat*, October 4, 1865.

16. John Peter Eddleman (1823–1901) was born in North Carolina and had moved to Rapides Parish by 1860. The census of that year shows him as a merchant at Huddleston. In October 1864, Eddleman was elected to the state legislature from Rapides Parish. He resigned his commission in January 1865. Eddleman moved his family to Orange County, Texas, at some time during the 1890s. Francis Reid, "My Eddleman Family," *Las Sabinas*, Vol. XXV, Book 3 (1998), 4–9; Population Schedules, Eighth Census, 1860, Rapides Parish, Louisiana.

17. Michael Ryan, a native of Ireland, had been a teacher and lawyer in Rapides Parish prior to the war. He had served in the state senate in the 1850s. Governor Wells appointed him district judge in June 1865. Whittington, *Rapides Parish*, 548; *Louisiana Democrat*, June 21, 1865.

1. Oliver Sanders was a thirty-three-year-old farmer born in Arkansas. Population Schedules, Eighth Census, 1860, Sabine Parish, Louisiana.

2. Joe Strather was probably Joseph T. Strother, a seventeen-year-old farm laborer. He was paroled at Alexandria on June 3, 1865, as a private in Company G, Second Louisiana Cavalry. Population Schedules, Eighth Census, 1860, Rapides Parish, Louisiana; C.S.R., M320, Roll 13. Alexander Strother had enlisted as a corporal in Todd's Prairie Rangers Cavalry company on November 1, 1862. He apparently deserted and joined the Jayhawkers. Lieutenant David Paul reported that his command captured Alexander Strother and two other Jayhawkers but had to shoot them when they tried to escape while being taken to Alexandria. C.S.R., M320, Roll 15; Lieut. David C. Paul to Maj. David F. Boyd, May 10, 1865, Brent Papers, LAGL.

3. Either Obediah Johnson, a twenty-year-old farm laborer, or Obediah Johnson, a forty-nine-year-old farmer. Population Schedules, Eighth Census, 1860, Rapides Parish, Louisiana.

4. Josiah Johnson was a fifty-year-old farmer living at Sugartown. His son Charles was nineteen years old. Budd may have been Josiah's twenty-three-year-old son Aaron. Population Schedules, Eighth Census, 1860, Calcasieu Parish, Louisiana.

5. Curley Johnson has not been identified.

6. Probably Eli M. Calcott, a twenty-eight-year-old merchant born in Mississippi. Population Schedules, Eighth Census, 1860, Rapides Parish, Louisiana.

7. Probably Robert Lynne, a lieutenant in Company E, Sixth Louisiana Infantry Regiment, who accompanied Patrick Keary to Louisiana and recruited a company for Keary's Battalion in Avoyelles Parish. The *New Orleans Times* reported on July 14, 1865, the following story: "A Captain Lynn was arrested in the City Hall yesterday by order of the Chief of Police, charged by several prominent citizens with committing a half dozen or more murders in the Parish of Avoyelles in 1863. It is reported that the Grand Jury of that Parish has found true bills against him for seventeen different capital offenses. His name was notorious through that country as a jayhawker." C.S.R., M320, Rolls 48, 169, 193; *Times*, July 14, 1865, quoted in *Opelousas Courier*, July 27, 1865.

8. Josiah Strother was an eighteen-year-old farm laborer. Population Schedules, Eighth Census, 1860, Rapides Parish, Louisiana.

9. Jeremiah Cloud was a twenty-eight-year-old farmer. He enlisted in Todd's Prairie Rangers cavalry company on November 1, 1862. A newspaper account about him read:

> "Captain Cloud has been in the woods and swamps about two years—but within the year he came in to Alexandria, and was put into

the rebel army. He got away and one day was captured in some way, and expected, of course, to swing; but one of his comrades begged him off on condition he should again join his company, which he did, but he did not stay joined. I said to him: 'But how did you get ammunition while in the swamps?'

"'We sent in a man now and then to join the rebel army, and when he got a good supply of cartridges he came out to us, and then we were very careful of it.'"

After deserting Todd's company, Cloud formed a company of Jayhawkers on the Calcasieu River and eventually commanded around sixty men. Confederate troops caught up with Cloud toward the end of the war and killed him, although whether this occurred in March or April 1865 is uncertain. Population Schedules, Eighth Census, 1860, Rapides Parish, Louisiana; C.S.R., M320, Roll 14; New Orleans *Era*, May 4, 1864; Paul to Boyd, March 27, 1865, Brent Papers, LAGL; *Opelousas Courier*, May 6, 1865.

10. Located on Spanish Lake between New Iberia and St. Martinville, Camp Pratt had been established in May 1862 as the camp of instruction for conscripts in south Louisiana. Vaughn Baker (ed.), "Glimpses of Iberia in the Civil War," *Attakapas Gazette* 6 (1971): 87; *O.R.*, XV, 756, 919.

11. Lieutenant Colonel Ross E. Burke, Second Louisiana Infantry Regiment, had been sent from his unit in Virginia to forward conscripts to that theater. General Richard Taylor assigned him to command Camp Pratt, which duty he carried out until relieved in December 1862. C.S.R., M320, Roll 103; *O.R.*, XV, 919.

12. Henry Wirz, Swiss by birth, had moved to Louisiana prior to the war and practiced medicine. He joined the Fourth Louisiana Infantry Battalion when the war began. In February 1864, he received appointment to superintend the prison at Andersonville, Georgia. Following the war, Union authorities tried Wirz and executed him in November 1865 for mistreating Union prisoners. Ella Lonn, *Foreigners in the Confederacy* (Chapel Hill: University of North Carolina Press, 1940), 273–75.

13. "Dog" Smith's identity has not been established firmly. A Captain George W. Smith, commanding a company of mounted men, operated against Jayhawkers in the area of Catahoula Lake in February 1864 using trail dogs. One source indicates that most of "Dog" Smith's men came from Bienville Parish. A history of Winn Parish states that Howard "Dog" Smith appeared in Winnfield in 1862 with a platoon of men to set up a home guard. He ousted the sheriff and took over full control of the parish. Smith brutalized people in the area. He had dogs named Old Rock and Ruler. Private William I. Bennett, Company I, Third Louisiana Infantry Regiment, while home on sick leave, ran Smith off and broke up his "gang" with the aid of local citizens. *O.R.*, XXXIV, Pt. 2, 976–77; *Biographical and Historical Memoirs of Northwest Louisiana*

(Nashville, Tenn.: Southern Publishing Co., 1890), 157; Richard Briley III, *Briley's Memorial History and Cemetery Directory of Winn Parish, Louisiana* (Montgomery, La.: Mid-South Publishers, 1966), 12–14.

14. Sandleford has not been identified.

Correspondence

1. John Routh Williams had served as captain of Company D, First Louisiana Cavalry Regiment until resigning October 23, 1862. In June 1865, Governor Wells appointed Williams as sheriff of Rapides Parish. C.S.R., M320, Roll 7; *Louisiana Democrat,* June 21, 1865.

2. The Louisiana legislature elected Governor Hahn to the United States Senate in January 1865, but that body never seated him. Amos E. Simpson and Vaughn Baker, "Michael Hahn: Steady Patriot," *Louisiana History* 13 (1972): 248.

3. Confederate soldiers frequently attempted to capture Wells and his sons. He told a congressional committee that he had to sleep in the woods, most of the time under guard. He claimed to have had from 30 to 160 Jayhawkers with him at various times. *House Reports,* 43rd Congress, 2nd Session, 1874–1875, No. 261, Pt. 3, 100.

4. Graham announced his candidacy for the Fourth Congressional District seat in October 1865. *Louisiana Democrat,* October 25, 1865.

5. Ferdinand L. Claiborne of Pointe Coupee Parish was one of the candidates for the congressional seat. *Louisiana Democrat,* September 6, 1865.

6. The 128th New York Infantry Regiment and the Third Massachusetts Cavalry Regiment went down Red River on May 7, 1864, and captured several wagonloads of corn for use by the army in Alexandria. Van Alstyne, *Diary of an Enlisted Man,* 318; Ewer, *The Third Massachusetts Cavalry,* 180.

7. Captain Dennis and his Jayhawkers have not been identified.

8. Thomas Woodward was a twenty-eight-year-old farm laborer born in Louisiana. Population Schedules, Eighth Census, 1860, Rapides Parish, Louisiana.

9. On May 9, 1865, Lieutenant David Paul's detachment captured Alexander Strother, Joseph McGuire, and David Davore, whom Paul called "notorious Jayhawkers." As Paul's men took them toward Alexandria, the three men tried to escape but were killed by their guards. Paul to Boyd, May 10, 1865, Brent Papers, LAGL.

10. William W. Smart and Lewis Texada represented Rapides Parish in the secession convention in January 1861. They voted in favor of Governor Moore's seizure of forts and other Federal property and for the ordinance of secession. *Official Journal of the Proceedings of the Convention,* 10, 20, 24.

11. The Confederate Congress passed the first conscription act in American history on April 16, 1862. The law made subject to military service

all white males between the ages of eighteen and thirty-five. An exemption act passed October 11, 1862, freed from conscription persons of various occupations including "one white man who was engaged exclusively in raising stock, for every 500 head of cattle, 250 head of horses or mules, or 500 head of sheep" and "one white man on each plantation of twenty or more negroes [*sic*]." This latter exemption became known popularly as the "twenty-nigger law." Albert B. Moore, *Conscription and Conflict in the Confederacy* (New York: Macmillan Co., 1924), 13, 68.

12. Major Eustace Surget had been Dick Taylor's brigade adjutant in Virginia and accompanied him to Louisiana as assistant adjutant-general and unofficial chief of staff. Richard Taylor, *Destruction and Reconstruction: Personal Experiences of the Late War*, ed. Richard B. Harwell (New York: Longmans, Green & Co., 1955), 49–50, 127.

13. No copies of the *Louisiana Democrat* for August 1863 still exist to confirm this statement.

14. General Taylor reported that large numbers of men from Brigadier General Henry H. Sibley's Texas cavalry brigade straggled off and returned home during the retreat to Opelousas. *O.R.*, XV, 394.

15. Dr. J. P. Davidson, a resident of Alexandria, gave a deposition which was included in a report by Thomas C. Manning to Governor Henry W. Allen on December 22, 1864. Davidson stated: "'Immediately on the occupation of the town by the Federal army, recruiting offices were opened for the enlistment of disaffected citizens into the service of the United States, under the title of "Louisiana Scouts," to whom a large bounty was offered. In a few days three companies of these men, (commonly called "jay-hawkers,") were organized, and placed under the command of men notorious for their resistance to the authority of the Confederate Government, and who burned with revenge against many of the loyal citizens of the parish. To these organizations was committed the patrolling of the country adjacent; they scoured it, visiting upon individuals their vengeance and vindictiveness. This irregular force entered the residences of planters, carrying off whatever they needed or could appropriate, and in many instances offering violence and insults. In the remote parts of the parish they burnt the dwellings of those who were supposed to have been active in pointing out or aiding in arresting conscripts. In one instance, within my knowledge, an attempt was made to confine the wife of one who had been somewhat active in designating the haunts of skulking conscripts, to the house, while they committed it to flames. After the army marched for Shreveport, something of order and quiet was enforced by Gen. Grover, the commandant of the post.'" *Official Report Relative to the Conduct of Federal Troops in Western Louisiana, During the Invasions of 1863 and 1864* (Shreveport, *La.*: News Printing Estab., 1865; reprint ed., Baton Rouge, La.: Otto Claitor, 1939), 69–70.

A Texas cavalry officer, who moved his company to a point on the road from Alexandria to Niblett's Bluff on the Sabine River some fifty to sixty miles from the latter point, made several reports to his superiors concerning conditions in the area. On one occasion he wrote: "The country is infested with Jayhawkers who are depredating upon the property of any person suspected of Southern feelings[.] In fact I am situated exactly as I would be in an enemies [*sic*] territory[.] . . . I have never seen such distress as exists among those who are friendly to us, and I must say that these are few—Their houses are way laid for the purpose of taking their lives, and their houses are plundered by armed bands in the day time, their negroes [*sic*] are run to Alexandria whether they desire to go or not. Every one has either to declare his adherence to the Yankee Government, leave their houses or die. . . ." Capt. John W. Slayton to Lt. F. H. Baily, April 14, 1864, in C.S.R., M323 (Texas Confederate Soldiers), Roll 212.

In another letter, the officer stated: "My camp is now full of Women, children, Negroes, Household plunder &c belonging to Southern men & families, who are here for protection from the Jayhawkers (alias Union cavalry)[.] They are all running from this region to Texas, [I]n 10 days I do not believe there will be a Southern family living in this section, [T]he Jayhawkers are Plundering and robbing them, I would like to have another company to chastise them, There are three organized companies of them that range between this point and Alexandria." Slayton to Capt. J. B. Turner, April 20, 1864, in C.S.R., M323 (Texas Confederate Soldiers), Roll 212.

A Northern newspaper correspondent, in writing about the men coming into Alexandria to join the Louisiana Scouts, confided to his readers, "Among them are some desperate men, and if occasionally a house is fired, or a private revenge is wreaked, I shall not be surprised." New Orleans *Era*, May 4, 1864.

16. No evidence of Haynes's service in any of the Seminole Wars has been found.

17. Todd's desertion in April 1864 and appointment to office in August 1865 are described in note 36 of chapter 1. After the war, a former lieutenant in Todd's company, Samuel Haas, wrote that Todd was an "imposter and not worth killing. . . . it would take a good size book to give his reputation as he was a deserter and one who went to the enemy as soon as he had a chance." Haas in another letter stated, "I was informed he [Todd] told some of the Co. if they ever got back to Chicot or Pine Prairie it was equal to a discharge." Many of Todd's men did desert and join the Jayhawkers. Samuel Haas to E. F. Brian, March 4, 1912, in Neville Johnson File, Confederate Pension Applications; Haas to Brian, August 12, 1912, in Neville Johnson File, Confederate Pension Applications.

18. E. E. Brooks was probably Enoch L. or Elisha L. Brooks, both of whom served in Haynes's Company B, First Louisiana Cavalry Scouts Battalion.

Clifton was probably Carlton S. G. Clifton, also of Haynes's company. Samuel N. Cain had been a farm laborer living at Sugartown; he later joined Haynes's company. Milam has not been identified. C.S.R., M396, Roll 11; Population Schedules, Eighth Census, 1860, Calcasieu Parish, Louisiana.

19. Probably Auguste Chevallier, a fifty-year-old farmer born in Louisiana. Population Schedules, Eighth Census, 1860, Rapides Parish, Louisiana.

20. Montfort Wells complained that James Madison Wells had confiscated some of his horses in March or April 1864. *Louisiana Democrat*, October 25, 1865.

Reconstruction of the States

1. John Stepney has not been identified.

2. E. F. Fitzgerald received an appointment as postmaster at Natchitoches. *Louisiana Democrat*, September 20, 1865.

3. William Pitt Kellogg was appointed by Lincoln as collector of the Port of New Orleans on April 13, 1865. He served until July 9, 1868, when he became a U.S. senator. U.S. Congress, *Biographical Directory of the American Congress, 1774–1971* (Washington, D.C.: Government Printing Office, 1971), 1219.

4. Robert W. Taliaferro was appointed postmaster at New Orleans on March 20, 1865, and served until July 30, 1868. Leonard V. Huber and Clarence A. Wagner, *The Great Mail: A Postal History of New Orleans* (State College, Pa.: American Philatelic Society, Inc., 1949), 115.

Rufus King Cutler had been a Confederate sympathizer early in the war but became a leading radical later. He represented Orleans Parish in the Constitutional Convention of 1864. The Union legislature elected him to the U.S. Senate in October 1864 but the latter body did not admit him. Francis P. Burns, "White Supremacy in the South: The Battle for Constitutional Government in New Orleans, July 30, 1866," *Louisiana Historical Quarterly* 18 (1935): 605; John Rose Ficklen, *History of Reconstruction in Louisiana (Through 1868)* (Gloucester, Mass.: Peter Smith, 1966 reprint), 90–91.

Benjamin F. Flanders was appointed special agent of the Treasury Department in Louisiana in 1863 and reappointed in 1866. *Biographical Directory of the American Congress*, 949.

BIBLIOGRAPHY

Primary Sources

Manuscripts

Appointment Book, 1873, Grant Parish Courthouse.

Barred and Disallowed Case Files of the Southern Claims Commission, 1871–1880, Record Group 233, Records of the U.S. House of Representatives, National Archives.

Priscilla M. Bond Diary, Louisiana and Lower Mississippi Valley Collection, LSU Libraries, Baton Rouge.

David F. Boyd Papers, Louisiana and Lower Mississippi Valley Collection, LSU Libraries, Baton Rouge.

Joseph L. Brent Papers, Louisiana Adjutant General's Library, Jackson Barracks, New Orleans.

Compiled Service Records of Confederate Soldiers Who Served in Organizations from the State of Louisiana, Microcopy 320, National Archives.

Compiled Service Records of Confederate Soldiers Who Served in Organizations from the State of Texas, Microcopy 323, National Archives.

Compiled Service Records of Volunteer Union Soldiers Who Served in Organizations from the State of Louisiana, Microcopy 396, Roll 11, National Archives.

Confederate Pension Applications, Louisiana State Archives and Records Service

Conveyance Book "T," Winn Parish Courthouse, Winnfield, Louisiana.

File 2055Vs1872, First Louisiana Independent Cavalry Scouts, Record Group 94, Records of the Adjutant General's Office, 1780s-1917, Volunteer Service Branch, National Archives.

D. E. Haynes, Box 13, U.S. Treasury Department, Records of the Secretary, Subseries 247e, Record Group 56, National Archives.

Dennis E. Haynes v. United States, U.S. Court of Claims, Congressional Jurisdiction Case #1745, Dennis E. Haynes, Box 298, 16E3/8/28/1, Record Group 123, National Archives.

Ker-Texada Papers, Manuscripts Department, Tulane University Archives, New Orleans.
Letters Received, Superintendent of Education, 1865–1877, Louisiana State Archives.
Letters Sent, Adjutant General's Office, Louisiana Militia, 1862–1865, Adjutant General's Library, Jackson Barracks, New Orleans.
Letters Sent Book, District of West Louisiana, January–February 1864, Ch. II, Vol. 75, Record Group 109, War Department Collection of Confederate Archives, National Archives.
Orders, Adjutant General's Office, Louisiana Militia, 174, Louisiana State Archives.
Population Schedules, Seventh Census, 1850, Lee County, Georgia, National Archives.
Population Schedules, Seventh Census, 1850, Rapides Parish, Sabine Parish, Louisiana.
Population Schedules, Eighth Census, 1860, Hardin County, Tyler County, Texas.
Population Schedules, Eighth Census, 1860, Rapides Parish, Calcasieu Parish, Madison Parish, St. Landry Parish, Pointe Coupee Parish, Sabine Parish, Louisiana.
Population Schedules, Ninth Census, 1870, Winn Parish, Louisiana.
Series 258, Applications for Assessor, Second District, Louisiana, Record Group 56, National Archives.
Tax Assessment Rolls, Winn Parish, 1869–1875, Louisiana State Archives and Records Service.
Texada Family Papers, 1855–1919, Tennessee State Library and Archives.
U.S. Treasury Department, Records of the Secretary, Subseries 247e, Record Group 56, National Archives.

Newspapers

Alexandria *Louisiana Democrat,* June 21, July 4, 18, 25, August 9, 16, September 20, October 18, 1865
Galveston *Weekly News,* July 20, 1864
Harper's Weekly, December 19, 1863; May 7, 1864
New Orleans *Daily Picayune,* March 12, 1863; December 11, 1864
New Orleans *Era,* November 21, 1863; May 4, 1864
New Orleans Times, March 1, March 2, April 10, 1864
Opelousas Courier, October 22, 1864; January 28, May 6, July 27, August 26, 1865

Secondary Works

Books

Beecher, Harris H. *Record of the 114th Regiment, N.Y.S.V.* Norwich, N.Y.: J. F. Hubbard Jr., 1866.

Biographical and Historical Memoirs of Northwest Louisiana. Nashville, Tenn.: Southern Publishing Co., 1890.

Briley, Richard, III. *Briley's Memorial History and Cemetery Directory of Winn Parish Louisiana.* Montgomery, La.: Mid-South Publishers, 1966.

Brown, Norman D. (ed.). *Journey to Pleasant Hill: The Civil War Letters of Captain Elijah P. Petty, Walker's Texas Division, C.S.A.* San Antonio: Institute of Texan Culture, 1982.

Carter, Howell. *A Cavalryman's Reminiscences of the Civil War.* New Orleans: American Printing Co., Ltd., 1900.

Currie, James T. *Enclave: Vicksburg and Her Plantations, 1863–1870.* Jackson: University Press of Mississippi, 1980.

Edwards, John N. *Noted Guerrillas, or the Warfare of the Border.* St. Louis: J. W. Marsh, 1880.

Evans, Clement A. (ed.). *Confederate Military History,* 10 vols. Atlanta: Confederate Publishing Co., 1899.

Ewer, Rev. James K. *The Third Massachusetts Cavalry in the War for the Union.* Maplewood, Mass.: William G. J. Perry Press, 1903.

Ficklin, John Rose. *History of Reconstruction in Louisiana (Through 1868).* Gloucester, Mass.: Peter Smith, 1966 reprint.

Futch, Catherine Baillio. *The Baillio Family.* Baton Rouge(?), 1961.

House Reports. 39th Congress, 1st Session, 1865–1866.

House Reports. 43rd Congress, 2nd Session, 1874–1875, No. 261, Pt. 3.

Howard, Perry H. *Political Tendencies in Louisiana.* Baton Rouge: Louisiana State University Press, 1971.

Huber, Leonard V., and Clarence A. Wagner. *The Great Mail: A Postal History of New Orleans.* State College, Pa.: American Philatelic Society, Inc., 1949.

Lonn, Ella. *Foreigners in the Confederacy.* Chapel Hill: University of North Carolina Press, 1940.

Moore, Albert B. *Conscription and Conflict in the Confederacy.* New York: Macmillan Co., 1924.

Northup, Solomon. *Twelve Years A Slave,* ed. Sue Eakin and Joseph Logsdon. Baton Rouge: Louisiana State University Press, 1968.

Official Army Register of the Volunteer Force of the United States Army for the Years 1861, '62, '63, '64, '65. 8 vols. and index. Washington, D.C.: Adjutant General's Office, 1865; reprint ed., Gaithersburg, Md.: Ron R. Van Sickle Military Books, 1987.

Official Journal of the Proceedings of the Convention of the State of Louisiana. New Orleans, La.: J. O. Nixon, Printer to the State Convention, 1861.

Official Report Relative to the Conduct of Federal Troops in Western Louisiana, During the Invasions of 1863 and 1864. Shreveport: News Printing Estab., 1865; reprint ed., Baton Rouge, La.: Otto Claitor, 1939.

Pellet, Elias P. *History of the 114th Regiment, New York State Volunteers*. Norwich, N.Y.: Telegraph & Chronicle Power Press Print, 1866.

Phisterer, Frederick (comp.). *New York in the War of the Rebellion, 1861 to 1865*, 5 vols. Albany, N.Y.: I. B. Lyon Co., 1912.

Reid, Maude. *Early Calcasieu Doctors, 1850–1912*. Lake Charles, La.: First National Bank, 1969.

Richardson, James D. *A Compilation of the Messages and Papers of the Presidents, 1789–1902*, 10 vols. Washington, D.C.: Bureau of National Literature and Art, 1903.

Scott, Walter. *Tales of a Grandfather: Being the History of Scotland*, ed. Edwin Ginn. Boston: Athenaeum Press, 1885.

Stafford, George M. G. *General Leroy Augustus Stafford: His Forebears and Descendants*. New Orleans: Pelican Publishing Co., 1943.

Stafford, George M. G. *The Wells Family of Louisiana and Allied Families*. Alexandria: Standard Printing Co., Inc., 1941.

Taylor, Richard. *Destruction and Reconstruction: Personal Experiences of the Late War*, ed. Richard B. Harwell. New York: Longmans, Green & Co., 1955.

U.S. Congress. *Biographical Directory of the American Congress, 1774–1971*. Washington, D.C.: Government Printing Office, 1971.

U.S. War Department. *War of the Rebellion: Official Records of the Union and Confederate Armies*, 128 parts in 70 vols. Washington, D.C.: Government Printing Office, 1880–1901.

Van Alstyne, Lawrence. *Diary of an Enlisted Man*. New Haven, Conn.: Tuttle, Morehouse & Taylor Co., 1910.

Wheat, James E. and Josiah. *Sketches of Tyler County History*. Bevil Oaks, Tex.: Whitmeyer Printing, 1986.

Whittington, G. P. *Rapides Parish, Louisiana: A History*. Baton Rouge, La.: Franklin Press, Inc., n.d.

Wiley, Bell I. (ed.). *"This Infernal War:" The Confederate Letters of Sgt. Edwin H. Fay*. Austin: University of Texas Press, 1958.

Williams, T. Harry. *Huey Long*. New York: Alfred A. Knopf, 1969.

Winters, John D. *The Civil War in Louisiana*. Baton Rouge: Louisiana State University Press, 1963.

Articles

Baker, Vaughn (ed.). "Glimpses of Iberia in the Civil War," *Attakapas Gazette* 6 (1971): 87.

Burns, Francis P. "White Supremacy in the South: The Battle for Constitutional Government in New Orleans, July 30, 1866," *Louisiana Historical Quarterly* 18 (1935): 605.

Lowrey, Walter M. "The Political Career of James Madison Wells," *Louisiana Historical Quarterly* 31 (1948): 1007.

Prichard, Walter (ed.). "A Tourist's Description of Louisiana in 1860," *Louisiana Historical Quarterly* 21 (1938): 1156.

Ragan, Cooper K. (ed.). "The Diary of Captain George W. O'Brien, 1863," *Southwestern Historical Quarterly* 67 (1963): 30–31, 45.

Reid, Francis. "My Eddleman Family," *Las Sabinas* 25, Book 3 (1998): 2–23.

Simpson, Amos E., and Vaughn Baker. "Michael Hahn: Steady Patriot," *Louisiana History* 13 (1972): 248.

INDEX

Adams, Joe, 6, 130n6
Alexandria, Louisiana, xvi, xviii, xix, xx, 7, 13, 19, 21, 25, 42, 43, 54–55, 56, 58, 59, 60, 61, 63, 65, 66, 75, 76, 77, 78, 79, 90, 91, 96, 97, 99, 100, 104, 105, 106, 109, 110, 123, 124, 126, 130n8, 143n1
Alexandria Louisiana Democrat, 99, 104, 106
Allen, Henry W., 55, 65, 104–5, 111, 143n14
Alton Penitentiary, 69
Americus, Georgia, 85
Ashe, Col. ——, 47
Ashe, Samuel D., 46, 141n4
Atchafalaya River, 45, 48, 62
Avoyelles Parish, Louisiana, 15

Baillio, Gervais, 62, 97, 145n5
Baillio, Mrs. Gervais, 62
Banks, Nathaniel P., xvi, xviii, 5, 7, 12, 31, 42, 54, 55, 56, 79, 99, 105, 130n1
Barker, Samuel, 70, 149n18
Barlow, J. H. C., 79, 151n13
Barracks Hospital (New Orleans), 63
Barrington, Henry, 7, 29–30
Bass, ——, 11, 83
Bass, Widow ——, 28
Baton Rouge, Louisiana, 65, 89, 108
Bayou Boeuf, 59, 97, 145n26
Bayou Courtableau, 45, 46
Bayou Fordoche, 48, 49, 51
Bayou Grossetete, 49, 50
Bayou Mallet, 35
Bayou Rapides, 96
Bayou Teche, 54
Bayou Teche campaign, 5, 42, 99, 130n1, 155n14
Belden, James K., 42, 140n9
Benjamin, Joseph, 65, 83, 88, 98, 147n21
Bevers, A. K., 57, 64, 143n17
Beyham, ——, 34
Bienville Parish, Louisiana, xix, 84–85, 86, 109
Blair, James D., 39, 41, 54, 56, 60, 140n4, 143n16
Bogan, John, Sr., 78, 90, 150n11
Boyce, ——, 105
Boyd, Levy, 10, 83, 134n25
Boyd, Sophia, 24–25, 35, 138n3
Brooks, Elisha L., 63, 78, 105, 146n11
Bruce, Robert, 25, 138n4
Bryant, Julian E., 68, 149n9
Bundick's Creek, 123
Burke, Ross E., 84, 153n11
Burt, Richard, 31–32, 139n18
Burton, Mrs. John J., 48, 141n6

Cain, Samuel N., 105, 157n18
Calcasieu Parish, Louisiana, 40, 43, 54, 57, 88, 123, 125
Calcasieu River, xvi, 8, 9, 12, 19, 25, 26, 34, 73, 77, 90
Calcott, Eli M., 83, 152n6
Camp Pratt, Louisiana, 84, 153n10
Carrier, Ursin, 34, 139n22

Carriere, Ozeme, 30, 34–36, 134n23, 139n13, 147n22
Carriere's Ferry, 34
Chambers, Josiah, 58, 83, 88, 144n20
Cheney, Lt. ——, 71
Cheneyville, Louisiana, 55
Chevallier, Auguste, 105, 157n19
City Hotel (New Orleans), 53
Claiborne, Ferdinand L., 95, 154n5
Clark, ——, 19
Clark, Augustus, 11, 135n32
Clark, George, 70–71
Clear Creek, 98
Clifton, Carlton S. G., 105, 123, 157n18
Cloud, Jeremiah, 84, 147n22, 152n9
Cloud, Noah, 26, 98, 138n6
Colfax Riot, xxi
Columbus, Georgia, 85
Commercial Hotel (New Orleans), 77
Confederate deserters, 5–6, 99
Conscription Act (Confederate), 98, 154n11
Constitutional Convention of 1864, 67, 148n1
Connelly, Elijah, 11, 83
Cooper Plantation, 71
Corley, Larkin D., 58, 64, 78, 90, 105, 144n21
Curtiss, Robert G., 69, 71, 149n11
Cutler, Rufus King, 112, 157n4
Cutlett, William, 49, 141n7

Dana, Napoleon J. T., 69, 149n13
Davis, Capt. ——, 9, 13
Davis, Jefferson, 118
Davore, David, 154n9
Dawes, Henry L., xix
Dennis, Capt. ——, 96
DeSoto Landing, Louisiana, 73
Deweese, Samuel, 68, 148n4
Dishroom, Capt. ——, 67, 148n3
Doyle, John, 28
Dudley, Dr. A. P., 10, 13, 54, 58, 83, 84, 133n22, 136n2, 142n6, 144n22, 147n22
Dugdemona River, xix
Dwight, William, 64, 146n14

Eddleman, John Peter, 80, 90, 135n28, 151n16
Elenor (steamer), 123

False River, 50
Farquhar, Dr. William, 30, 40, 105, 139n12
Fassman's Press (New Orleans), 64
Field, Alexander P., xix
Fitch, John S., 45, 141n2
Fitzgerald, E. F., 110, 157n2
Flanders, Benjamin F., xix, 102, 112, 157n4
Flowers, Clara, 61, 145n2
Flyn, Bob, 8, 99
Fontaine, Juste, 64, 65, 146n13
forts
  Bisland, 130n1, 131n12
  DeRussy, 55, 142n10
Fournet, Valsin A., 8, 131n12, 131n16
Franklin, Louisiana, xvii, xviii, 38, 53, 54
Franklin, William B., 54, 142n8
Freemasons, 14, 140n9

Goolsby, Lazarus, 7
Graham, C. E., 24, 138n2
Graham, George M., 79–80, 90, 92, 94, 95–96, 101, 109, 151n15, 154n4
Grant, Ulysses S., xix, xxi
Grant Parish, Louisiana, xxi
Graves, R. W., 70, 149n16
Green, Uriah, 10, 133n23
Grover, Cuvier, 59, 96, 100, 144n23
Groves, James P., 10, 83, 134n27
Gunter, Jacob, 13, 83, 136n1
Gyder, John, 70–72, 149n19

Hahn, Michael, 89, 102, 136n37, 154n2
Hamilton, Andrew Jackson, xviii, 53, 54, 102, 142n1
Hardin County, Texas, xvi, 5–6
Hardin Court House, 6–7
Harrison, Isaac F., 67, 72, 148n2
Hawkins, John P., 66, 77, 78, 112, 148n23
Hawthorne, Albert, 58, 64, 105, 144n21
Haynes, Benjamin F., xxi
Haynes, Elizabeth Swearingen, xv, 14, 24–25, 27, 28, 59–60, 63, 68, 73–74, 97, 100
Haynes, Patrick, xix, xxi
Haynes, Permilia Dean, xix
Haynes, William, xxi, 14–15, 68
Haynes, Zelenor, xxi
Hebert, Victor, 51, 141n8
Headrick, P., 67, 148n3
Henry Von Phul (steamer), 76
Hickory Branch, 125
Hickory Flat, Louisiana, 84
Hineston, Louisiana, 8, 13–14, 15, 21, 23, 24, 28, 35, 90, 98, 99
Hubbard, George C., 39, 54, 140n3

Iles, ——, 30
Iles, Dempsey, 40, 140n7
Ivey, William E., 23–24, 26, 27, 58, 60, 65, 77, 83, 88, 98, 99, 138n1

Jayhawkers, xvii, xviii, 9, 12, 15, 23, 40, 54, 55, 89, 92, 106, 143n11, 145n1, 147n20, 147n21, 147n22, 153n9, 154n3, 155n15
Johnson, ——, 28, 138n8
Johnson, ——, 77
Johnson, Aaron, 83, 152n4
Johnson, Andrew, xix, 56, 107, 143n13
Johnson, Charles, 83, 152n4
Johnson, Curley, 83
Johnson, Josiah, 40, 83, 140n7, 152n4
Johnson, Obediah, 83, 152n3
Jones, ——, 32
Jones, Carroll, 15, 83, 137n9
Jones, Charles H., 13–14, 136n3
Jumel, Allen, 45, 141n1

Keary, Helen, 14, 137n6
Keary, Patrick F., 13–16, 23, 136n4
Keily, Daniel J., 64, 65, 146n12
Kellogg, William Pitt, 112, 157n3
Know-Nothings, 16

Lanacoco Prairie, Louisiana, 10, 15, 24, 80
Lee, Sgt. ——, 17–18
Lee, Surgeon ——, 62–63
Lincoln, Abraham, 6
Little Tensas Bayou, 70
Loftus, Patrick J., 16, 137n11
Long, Huey P., Jr., xix
Long, Huey P., Sr., xx
Long, John M., xix, xx
Louisiana troops (Confederate)
  cavalry—regiments: 2nd, 39, 41, 45, 56, 143n15; 3rd, 135n36, 148n2; 6th, 134n24, 138n1
  infantry—battalions: 10th (Yellow Jacket), 8, 98, 99, 131n12; Keary's, 13–18, 20, 82, 136n4, 152n7
Louisiana troops (Union)
  cavalry—regiments: 1st, 61, 145n3, 146n18; 2nd, xx, 64, 65, 146n12, 146n15, 146n18
  cavalry—battalions: 1st Scouts, xviii, 57, 61, 62, 63, 64, 72, 87, 89, 92, 107–8, 111, 143n17, 146n15, 155n15
Lovin, ——, 11
Loving, J. W., 10, 84, 134n25
Lusk, S. A., 67, 148n3
Lynch, Matthew, 26, 138n5

Lynne, Robert, 83, 152n7
Lyon, T. Lytt, 46, 141n3

Madison Parish, Louisiana, xviii, 67–68, 76
Maltby, Jasper A., 75, 150n1
Mansfield (Sabine Crossroads), Battle of, 59, 62, 64, 145n8
Mansura, Engagement at, 62, 145n6
Many, Louisiana, 15, 17, 18, 82
Marksville, Louisiana, 62
Martin, Robert Washington, 10–12, 15, 19, 23, 24, 26, 29, 55, 58, 60, 61, 65, 80, 82–83, 84, 86, 88, 98, 99, 113, 124, 134n24
Massachusetts troops
cavalry—regiments: 3nd, 96, 154n6
McCallister, ——, 73
McCormick, John, 39, 140n2
McCullough, ——, 72–73
McGuire, Joseph, 154n9
McNutt, Anderson, 77, 150n7
Milam, ——, 105
Milliken's Bend, Louisiana, 67, 68, 72
Mississippi River, xvii, 63, 72
Moody, S. N., 142n2
Moody's Store (New Orleans), 53
Moore, Thomas O., 62, 97, 145n4
Morea, Mr. ——, 69
Morgan's Ferry, 48
Morganza, Louisiana, 45
Mount Lebanon, Louisiana, 84
Mouton, Jean Jacques Alfred Alexandre, 8, 83
Mower, Joseph A., 62, 145n7

Natchez, Mississippi, 65, 89, 108
Natchitoches, Louisiana, 12, 18, 84, 110
Natchitoches Parish, Louisiana 11, 85
Navigator (steamer), 110
New Iberia, Louisiana, 36, 37, 38, 40, 41, 45, 56, 60
New Orleans, Louisiana, xvi, xviii, xix, xx, xxi, 12, 31, 53, 54, 59, 62, 65, 68, 75, 76, 79, 89, 102, 103, 106, 108, 110, 111, 123, 124
New Orleans Times, 87
New York troops
infantry—regiments: 114th, 38; 128th, 96, 154n6; 165th, 39, 54
Niblett's Bluff, Texas, 28
Nicaragua, xv, 9, 101
Nichols, Mary Jane, 9, 24, 28, 59, 133n21
Nichols, Simon C., 9, 133n21

O'Brien, John, 40–41, 43, 56, 60
Opelousas, Louisiana, 12, 30, 33, 34, 35, 45, 105

Parham, William S., 149n20
Parham's Plantation, 70
Parker, Benjamin F., 8, 131n14
Parker, James, 8, 99, 131n13
Parker Plantation, 70
Paul, David C., 65, 83, 88, 98, 136n2, 147n20, 154n9
Pedro, Levi, 28
Peek's Ferry, 48
Perkins, Hannah, 77, 150n8
Pharris, Green, 31–32, 139n16
Phelps, Josiah, 6–7, 130n4
Pierce, Bishop ——, 85
Pierce, Dr. Lovick, 85
Pineville, Louisiana, xviii, 59, 90, 92, 109
Polk, Mrs. William, 100
Polk's Bridge, 59, 97, 145n26
Pollard, —— (Caswell F. or John D.), 31, 139n15
Pollard, Mrs. ——, 31
Port Hudson, Louisiana, xvii, 7, 28, 40, 45, 46, 48, 50, 51, 130n8
Presidential Amnesty Proclamation of May 19, 1865, 55–56, 143n13

Presidential Proclamation of
December 8, 1863, 55, 143n12
Presley, Bryant, 10, 84, 134n25
Presswood, Austin, 8, 13, 131n11

Rapides Parish, Louisiana, xv, xvi, xviii, xx, 8, 10, 11, 14, 39, 55, 57, 58, 73, 77, 87, 92, 93, 94, 95, 99, 101, 104, 105, 107
Rawhide, Louisiana, 83
Red River, 31, 55, 60, 63, 65, 84, 107, 109, 113
Red River Campaign, 1863, xvii
Red River Campaign, 1864, xviii, xx
Richardson, E. D., 68
Richardson, William A., xxi
Roussou, ——, 24
Ryan, Michael, 80, 90, 94, 96, 151n17

Sabine Parish, Louisiana, 15, 82
Sabine Pass, xvii
Sanders, Nathaniel, 29, 139n11
Sanders, Oliver, 82–83, 152n1
Sandersville, Louisiana, 29
Sandleford, ——, 84
Scarbrock, Francis Van, 9, 133n19
Seminole War, xv, 101
Shannon, David R., 58, 144n19
Shehane, ——, 85
Sheridan, Philip H., 76, 150n5
Sherman, Francis T., 76, 103, 150n4
Ship Island, Mississippi, 100
Shreveport, Louisiana, xvii, 15, 17, 18, 19, 82
Simmons, William, 32, 33, 139n21
Six Mile Creek, 29, 124–26
Slocum, Henry W., 76, 150n2
small pox, 38
Smart, Dr. E. E., 10, 65, 83, 88, 134n26
Smart, Reese W., 10, 65, 83, 88, 134n26
Smart, William W., 10, 58, 65, 83, 88, 98, 134n26, 154n10
Smith, ——, 43
Smith, Andrew J., 55, 62, 143n10
Smith, Archibald, 19–21, 23, 79, 90, 99, 137n14
Smith, Capt. "Dog," 84, 86, 113, 153n13
Smith, Edmund Kirby, 15, 65, 101, 137n8
Smith, George A., 10, 135n28
"Soldier's Home" (New Orleans), 54
Southern Claims Commission, xx
Spaight, Ashley W., 130n2
Spanish Lake (Caddo Parish), 19
Stafford, Thomas J., 39, 59–60, 79, 140n5
Stephens, Chase A., 115
Stepney, John, 110
St. James Hospital (New Orleans), 62, 145n9
St. Martin Parish, Louisiana, 84
St. Martinville, Louisiana, 38, 40
Stock Landing (Mississippi River), 63
Stone, Charles P., 54, 142n7
Strather's Bridge, 9
Strother, Alexander, 83, 136n1, 147n22, 152n2, 154n9
Strother, Joseph T., 83, 152n2
Strother, Josiah, 84, 152n8
Sugartown, Louisiana, 28, 40, 123–26
Sumner, Charles, 112
Surget, Eustace, 99, 155n12
Swan, Charley, 68, 72–73
Swan, Hop (Appleton G. ?), 24, 138n2
Swan, John J., 24, 31, 138n2
Swearingen, E. A., 54, 63, 142n3
Sweat, Isaac, 24, 138n2

Taylor, Richard, 5, 14, 42, 46, 55, 65, 83, 85, 89, 98, 99, 108, 130n1
Taylor, W. W., 24, 138n2
Ten Mile Creek, 126
Texada, Joseph, 79, 90, 150n12
Texada, Lewis, 55, 98, 143n11, 154n10

Texas troops (Confederate)
artillery—batteries:
Edgar's, 143n15
cavalry—regiments: 13th, 136n3
infantry—battalions: 11th, 5, 130n1
Walker's Infantry Division, 9, 133n17
Texas troops (Union)
cavalry—regiments: 1st, xvi
Thomas, Samuel, 68–69, 71–72, 148n8
Todd, Samuel M., 12, 55, 105, 135n36, 156n17
Twiggs County, Georgia, 30
Tyler County, Texas, xv, xix, xxi, 6, 13

Union sympathizers, xvi, 6–7, 8, 11–12, 24, 26, 27, 30, 45, 55, 57–58, 65, 93, 98, 105, 108
Union troops
Nineteenth Army Corps, 54, 55, 142n8
Sixteenth Army Corps, 55, 143n10
cavalry—regiments: 2nd, 123
infantry—regiments: 46th United States Colored, 69, 149n10; 49th United States Colored, 148n6; 64th United States Colored, 148n8
United States Mutual Protection Company, 115
U. S. Court of Claims, xx

Vanchaux, Jerry, 20, 23, 79, 90, 137n15
Van Vleck, George W., 6, 130n7
Vermillion Bayou, 41
Vermillionville, Louisiana, 41, 43, 45, 60
Vicksburg, Mississippi, 34, 68, 71, 72, 73, 75
Vicksburg Planters' Association, 72
Vincent, William G., 43, 140n10

Walker, John G., 9, 30
Walker, William, xv, 9
Walley, ——, 10–11, 98
Walnut Bayou, 70
Warmoth, Henry Clay, xxi
Washington, D.C., xix, 88, 107, 111, 113, 115
Washington, Louisiana, 36, 45, 46, 47
Watt, ——, 72
Weeks, J. A., 147n21
Wells, James Madison, xviii, 10, 11, 12, 54, 55, 56, 59, 67, 76, 77, 87, 92–93, 102, 103, 104, 110, 113, 135n29, 135n35, 142n5, 154n3
Wells, Levi, 106
Wells, Susan, 70, 149n17
Wells, Thomas Montfort, 76, 106, 150n3, 157n20
Wetherford, Alfred, 9, 105, 133n18
Wetherford, Rollin, 28
Whiskey Chitto Creek, 32, 33, 139n19
White, James G., 79, 109, 151n14
Whittaker, William A., 41, 43, 140n9, 141n12
Willett, Charles H., 58, 105, 144n21
Williams, John Routh, 87, 154n1
Williamson, Henry F., xx, 61, 64–65, 145n3
Winn Parish, Louisiana, xix, xxi, 84
Wirz, Henry, 84, 153n12
Woodard, Thomas, 96, 154n8
Woodville, Texas, 13

Yellow Bayou, Battle of, 62
Young, Paul, 31, 33, 139n17
Young, Van E., 68, 148n6
Young's Point, Louisiana, 72, 73